Son of Two Bloods

Winner of the
1995
North American
Indian Prose Award

Award Committee

Gerald Vizenor, Chairman
University of California at Berkeley

Diane Glancy
Macalester College

Louis Owens
University of New Mexico at Albuquerque

A. LaVonne Brown Ruoff
University of Illinois at Chicago

Son of Two Bloods

VINCENT L. MENDOZA

University of Nebraska Press
Lincoln and London

© 1996 by the University of Nebraska Press

All rights reserved

Manufactured in the United States of America

⊛ The paper in this book meets the minimum requirements of American National Standard for Information Sciences—Permanence of Paper for Printed Library Materials, ANSI Z39.48-1984.

Library of Congress Cataloging-in-Publication Data

Mendoza, Vincent L. (Vincent Leon), 1947–

Son of two bloods / Vincent L. Mendoza.

p.   cm.

ISBN 0-8032-3188-1 (cl : alk. paper)

1. Mendoza, Vincent L. (Vincent Leon), 1947–   . 2. Creek Indians—Biography.
3. Creek Indians—Mixed descent.   4. Creek Indians—Social conditions.   I. Title.

E99.C9M435   1996

973'.04973—dc20

[B]

95-50326

CIP

Dedicated with love
to my grandchildren, Terri and Bryson

Contents

Illustrations

Following page 74

Great-grandfather Temiye Kernels
Blas Mendoza, 1929
Great-grandparents Alex and Martha McIntosh with their children
Martha and Concho Mendoza, 1942
Junior, Dad, Linda, and Vince
Mom and Grandma McIntosh
Claude Mendoza and His Mariachis
Charlie and Concho Mendoza
Linda Mendoza Dellinger
Vincent Mendoza, Phu Bai, 1968
Deborah Chelf Mendoza
Vincent and Debbie Mendoza, 1970
Felicia Ann Mendoza and Micaela Mendoza
Micaela Mendoza
Debbie and Terri
Lance Anthony DeGraw
Felicia and Terri
Vincent Mendoza, 1994

Acknowledgments

I thank my wife Alice, my best friend, for her support. A special thanks to my good friend Betty Donohue for her guidance and enthusiasm. To Louis Owens, a very special thank you for your direction. To Connie Perez, Charles Mendoza, and Ray Mendoza, many thanks for your help. To my guardian spirit: mado (thank you) for all you have given me.

Son of Two Bloods

ONE // **The Blood**

As a four-year-old, I sat in the backseat of the old Chevrolet. All was quiet as we drove through the night toward Claremore, Oklahoma. I looked out the window at the thousands of stars in the sky. My father, Concho Mendoza, drove without speaking. My mother sniffled into her hanky, trying to be quiet, more concerned about me than herself. My great-grandmother, Sissy Kernels, lay near death at the Claremore Indian Hospital; she had asked to see me. A full-blood Creek, she spoke not a word of English. She couldn't even pronounce my name, Vincent, she could only call me "Benji," and I called her "Little Grandma." I called her that because she stood no more than four feet, eight inches tall. My grandmother, Annie McIntosh, had translated "Little Grandma" to her, and this pleased her. I remember her toothless smile and her sparkling eyes. Her dark, wrinkled hands would hold mine and pat them as if they were dough and she could mold them into anything she wished. Though we could not understand each other there was this sense of love between us. She would look at me and smile, then nod her head. I in turn would pat her hand, or hug her, or ask childish questions like "How old are you?" or "Where'd your teeth go?" Or sometimes when I got a tad hyper I'd stick my tongue out at her or make a face and she would cackle, then say something to Grandmother and Mama, then all three would laugh. I loved my Little Grandma, we had fun together. I remember hearing Mama and Grandma McIntosh talking about Little Grandma. She had been a little girl in November 1861 when Chief Opothleyahola took his people, the "Loyal Creeks," north to Kansas. They were being pursued by Confederate troops. Little Grandma could only remember the crying. She would always hear the crying.

The first thing I noticed as I entered the large white room was a doctor. He was tall, wore glasses and a white coat. He had a thing around his neck that doctors used to make you cold when they poked it on your chest, or your back. He was old like the rest of the big people in the room. I knew this because most of his hair was gone, and what was left was gray as cement. Next to him stood a nurse. She looked at me without any expression. I didn't look at her for long, because nurses gave shots, and I didn't want her getting any ideas. I smiled as I saw my Grandma and Grandpa McIntosh. Grandma smiled at me, while Grandpa showed no expression. It was then I noticed that they all stood around a real high bed. It was the tallest bed I had ever seen and I wondered who in the world would want such a bed. Then Mama spoke to me, "Vincent, do you want to see Little Grandma?"

"Sure, Mama, where is she?"

"She's right there on the bed, baby."

I jumped as high as I could but couldn't really see her. It was then I heard a chair being scooted across the dull white linoleum floor. I climbed on the chair and in an instant was crawling across the sheets toward my great-grandmother. She looked like she was asleep. I kissed her on the lips and called her name, "Little Grandma, Little Grandma, wake up."

Her eyes were still closed. "Benji," she said. She smiled, then ever so slowly she opened her eyes. "Benji."

"I love you, Little Grandma, get well," I said. Grandma McIntosh translated my words.

"Benji," she said, and as I looked into her eyes I could see the sparkle reappear. I kissed her once more and then I heard the doctor tell my mother that it was time to leave. Little Grandma closed her eyes and breathed deeply as Mama helped me down from the bed.

The next morning I heard Mama talking on the phone. She sounded excited and when I looked at her she smiled. She hung up the phone and then called me over to her. "Little Grandma is doing fine. The doctors think it was a miracle or something, because she woke up this morning hungry, and all her vital signs are normal. She's doing fine, baby."

I could hardly wait until we could play together again, but right now I knew Little Grandma was just tired. I was sure that I would see her again soon.

Weeks went by, or months. Mama gave me a bath in an old metal tub we had in the kitchen. We were going to see Little Grandma again and she wanted me to look nice. I assured her that Little Grandma wouldn't care if I was dirty or not, but she insisted that I be clean. Besides she was bigger than me.

I piled into the backseat with my older sister, Linda, and my older brother, Junior. Junior was ten years old and Linda was nine. Junior was a deaf-mute and Linda was just a nuisance. Her sole purpose in life was to tattle on me. Anyway, we were all dressed to kill. Mama and Daddy got in the car and we began our journey to a place called Sapulpa. It was dark by the time we got there. As we stepped from the car I could hear a hymn being sung in the Creek language. Mama quickly ushered us into a small house called a camp house. I saw my uncles and aunts and my cousins, but I remained close to Mama. She said I had to wait awhile, and I walked away and stood by the door. From the door I could see the white church. The Creek songs were coming from the church, and yellow light from the church windows shone in the dark. Just then my cousin Butch LaSarge whispered in my ear, "I know where Little Grandma is."

"Where, Butch?"

"Over yonder, in the church, but you gotta be quiet cause she's sleeping."

"Let's go see her!" I replied, and faster than slick we were out the door and running through the darkness toward the bright lights of the church.

We went through a door at the very front of the church, where the preacher would normally enter. We stopped and stared at all the people singing. They were all Indians, some darker than others, some mixed bloods. I looked about and saw a funny-shaped box with a lid that was open. As I examined it I could barely see just the tip of someone's nose. I jumped up and down, trying to catch a glimpse of who was in the funny-shaped box. Seeing an empty chair I pulled it close to the funny box and climbed on it for a better look. I couldn't believe my eyes. It was Little Grandma, and she was asleep. I touched her shoulder gently but she didn't respond to my touch. "Little Grandma wake up, it's me, Benji." She still didn't move or notice me. She lay perfectly still, and I knew that she must be real tired. Then I felt a strong arm about my waist and found myself being lifted from the chair and placed on the wooden floor of the Indian Baptist Church. I looked up into the dark face of an old man. "That's my Little Grandma," I said.

"She's sleeping, boy," he said quietly.

I nodded my head at him. "I'll come back when she wakes up."

"That's good" was all he said.

I turned and headed for the same door that I had entered. I stopped at the door and looked back at the funny-shaped box once again, and I wished I could hug Little Grandma one more time. But then I remembered that she was sleeping and I turned and stepped into the darkness. I ran like the wind toward the camp house. I felt good.

I was born on 5 September 1947 in Tulsa, Oklahoma, to Consepcion and Martha Mendoza. I was given my name by my father. He named me Vincent for the patron saint, and Leon after Leon McAuliffe, a steel guitarist in the "Bob Wills Band." God, I hated my name! But Dad being Dad, and a musician, named me after an entertainer. In retrospect, I was certainly glad that Dad wasn't an aviator, or I would have surely been named Orville or Wilbur.

Dad's parents, Blas and Ramona Mendoza, came from Mexico. He was from San Luis Potosi, and she from Zacatecas, Zacatecas (a state and city with the same name, comparable to Oklahoma City, Oklahoma). Her maiden name was Rosales, she came from a wealthy family. She knew only the best, attending private schools until kidnapped at the age of twelve by my Grandfather Blas. Blas was fifteen when he kidnapped Grandma, and in 1904 they crossed the border legally at El Paso. They traveled north doing migrant work where they could, and in 1916 in Alva, Texas, my father, Consepcion (nicknamed Concho), was born. Grandmother gave birth to fifteen children, but only four survived. Claude was the oldest, then Dad, Frank, and Consuela. During the late 1920s the Mendoza family worked in the coal mines at Hartshorne, Oklahoma. It was there that Dad was taught to play the saxophone by a white miner. Soon the Mendoza family was famous for their mariachi music. Blas played the guitar, Claude the fiddle, Dad the sax, and cousin Charlie the bass. The family moved to Tulsa in the early 1930s to work the coal mines in that area. In 1938 Dad and his cousin Willie went to a Bob Wills dance at the well-known Cains' Ballroom, where he asked the prettiest girl he had ever seen to dance. Her name was Martha Mae McIntosh.

Martha Mae McIntosh was born 24 October 1916 in Hitchita, Oklahoma, to Newman and Annie McIntosh. Newman was born to Alex and Martha Hawkins McIntosh, and Annie to Temiye and Sissy McGilbra Kernels. Martha went to school at Hitchita, and when she and her siblings grew older they attended Chilocco Indian Agricultural School, near Ponca City. My mother had four brothers and one sister. Tandy was the oldest brother. He was killed at Salerno, Italy, during World War II, when Oklahoma's Forty-fifth Division stormed ashore there in September

1943. Next was Mama, then Solomon, who gained fame as a boxer from Chilocco. He won the state and regional titles, only to lose in Madison Square Garden. He was later killed in a car accident. Then Sam, who was my favorite uncle. He was funny. He talked a mile a minute, and everyone laughed at his stories. He was a cowboy at heart, he even owned a white horse. Next was Bill. I liked Bill, he had a cool voice and I loved to hear him talk and laugh. He always told me stories about the Navy, and the way he described things, it was almost like being there with him. Uncle Bill was cool. And last but certainly not least was Aunt Lucy, the baby of the family. I loved it when Aunt Lucy and Uncle Burban would visit us in Tulsa, she was always so happy and carefree, and I wished that she lived in Tulsa. After her graduation Mama had moved to Tulsa and worked as a nanny. It was in Tulsa that she and her best friend from Chilocco, Evelyn Duncan, went to a dance at Cains' Ballroom. They paid thirty-five cents each. It was there that she met a handsome young Mexican boy by the name of Concho Mendoza.

We lived on the north side of Tulsa. Mama told me that we lived on North Rockford, near the intersection of Independence and Rockford. That one street was my world, and I knew every inch of it as if it belonged to me. The larger streets I had been told were North Peoria and North Utica. Mama made me promise to never ever cross these streets, or I would get run over like a dog, and I had seen run-over dogs before and didn't like the possibility of lying in the street with my tongue hanging out.

I heard the kids next door and walked to the door. They had just come home from school, and soon I too would go to school. I had heard Mama talking to the neighbors about me going to school in September. I opened the screen door and stepped out with my diaper and cowboy boots on. Mama still dressed me like a baby, and boy, did I catch heck from the other kids. The family that lived next door to us were really nice. They nicknamed me "Cano," short for Mexicano, and they called my brother "Nuno," but I don't know why. Their skin was brown too, and they treated me like their little brother. No one would pick on me as long as Luey, John, or David Bargas was around.

Most of the Mexican people I knew lived in that area. It was nice, and we were all happy. My family lived in a three-room house that my Dad rented from Mr. Bargas. We had a living room, a bedroom, and a kitchen. We had a toilet too. It was plumbed, but it was outside in a small outhouse. I hated it because it smelled awful. Our neighbors on the south side of us were the Archueletas. Moses, Sonya, and their daughter Rose, who was seven years old. They liked me and I liked them, and besides they had the only television in the entire neighborhood. Kids would be lined out the door on Saturday morning, and Sonya Archueleta would see to it that I got to cut in line. She and Mrs. Bargas were the two nicest ladies in the whole world, next to my mama.

I got sick one day, and then everything got kind of fuzzy. I could hear people talking, but I couldn't open my eyes for some reason. I heard the strange word "pneumonia," but I didn't know what that was. I guess I slept for days, then finally I opened my eyes, but I couldn't see too well. I was somewhere, but it sure wasn't my bed. I was in a see-through bag of some kind. I saw a lady dressed in a long black robe with a white collar around her whole face and neck. She smiled when I looked at her. "I'm Sister Mary Francis," she said. I tried to speak but couldn't, so I just nodded my head a little. She turned to speak to another lady dressed like her. "I'm not going to let this baby die!" she said loudly, and she reached down and yanked the see-through bag off of me. I felt her pick me up in her arms, and then that's all I remember. When I awoke, I was home in my bed. "Mama, I'm thirsty," I yelled. Mama came running in from the kitchen. I looked into her smiling face, "Am I dead, Mama?" Tears streamed from her eyes. "No, baby, you're not dead. You're not ever going to die," she said as she hugged me.

I heard a noise and slowly made my way out of bed and into the living room. To my surprise I saw a large television set sitting in our living room. "Mama, we have a television!" I yelled. Mama stooped down to me. "Daddy and I bought it just for you, baby." I looked into her pretty face, "Thanks, Mama," then I hugged her.

Friday night arrived, and after supper we all got into our black Chevrolet and Dad drove us to my Uncle Claude's house. Uncle Claude was the leader of the family band. Dad played soprano saxophone, Uncle Claude played the fiddle, their cousin Charlie played the stand-up bass, and a friend of theirs, John Segovia, played the guitar. If this music was Mexican music, then I guess I was for sure a Mexican. I loved every beat that I heard. I would sit in front of them and listen to their music for hours. Chachas, rumbas, rancheras, boleros, corridos, and waltzes, they could play anything. Charlie would smile at me or wink as I watched his fingers pluck the strings of the bass to the beat of the music. Most of all I enjoyed listening to my Uncle Claude sing. He was short and round, but his voice was pleasing to the ear and I could hardly wait to hear him sing another song. This was better than radio any day. I only had one problem. I couldn't understand what he was singing, because he sang in Spanish. My mother, Martha, was almost full-blood Creek Indian, and Dad was full-blood Mexican. That left me with one foot on the boat and the other on the dock. I figured I'd work things out sooner or later, but right now I was going to enjoy some of my Aunt Julia's tamales and strawberry pop. I loved it when the band practiced, and I figured I was one lucky kid getting to hear all that music for free.

September arrived and I helped my brother pack. It was time for Junior to go off to a school for the deaf. Mama told me that when he was almost three years old he took a high fever for several days. The doctor believed it was something called "meningitis." After the fever broke, Junior was deaf and no longer talked. We took him to the bus station in downtown Tulsa, where he met several other deaf kids, all going to a place called the Oklahoma School for the Deaf at Sulphur, Oklahoma. I waved at my brother as he smiled and waved to us from the bus window, and I choked on the fumes from the bus as it slowly pulled away from the depot. I looked up at Mama, she was crying as she waved goodbye to Junior, then we all walked quietly back to the car and went home.

The next morning Mama dressed me for school. She had bought me some blue jeans and a new blue shirt with red and yellow rockets on it. I thought I was all dressed up, no more diapers for this guy, no siree. I put on my new socks and then Mama helped me put on my old cowboy boots, and soon we were walking down Independence Street toward Lowell Elementary School. I looked forward to school, I mean all the other kids went to school, I figured I could handle it too. We walked into the schoolyard and then Mama opened a real big door and we stepped into a long hallway. "What's that smell, Mama?"

"It's wax and polish, baby."

I breathed deeply. It smelled clean and fresh, so far so good, I thought. Mama opened the door to a room and we went in. Boy, there were kids my size all over the place. They were running and screaming and having a grand old time. I could hardly wait to cut loose with a yell of my own. An old woman sat at a desk; when she saw me and Mama she smiled, then stood and walked over to us.

"Hello," she said to Mama, "I'm Mrs. Smith."

"I'm Mrs. Mendoza and this is Vincent."

The old lady called Mrs. Smith leaned way down and looked into my face, "Hello, Vincent," she said.

I looked into her wrinkled old face. She wore glasses, and she had gray hair and bushy black eyebrows and a black mustache! I stared in disbelief. I had never, ever, seen a woman with a black mustache. It wasn't thick like my Uncle Joe's, in fact it was kind of thin, but there was hair on her upper lip! I tugged on Mama's skirt. Mama leaned down and I whispered in her ear, "Mama, she's got a mustache!" Mama smiled. "Go play, Vincent," she said.

"Yes, Vincent, go play," Mrs. Hairy Lip said, and I slowly walked toward the indoor jungle gym. I had started to pull myself up on it when I stopped to turn and look at Mama. To my surprise she was just walking out the door. I sprinted for the door as fast as I could run and caught up with her before she could get too far down the hallway. "Mama, wait for me!"

Mama stopped and turned around. She knelt down as I ran to her.

"Mama, don't leave me here. I want to go home!"

"Vincent, don't you want to be a big boy like Luey, John, and David?"

"Yes, Mama, I sure do, but I don't want to stay here."

"Luey, John, and David all went to school here, and Mrs. Smith taught them how to be good. So you march back in there and mind what Mrs. Smith says. And someday you'll be a big boy just like the Bargas boys, okay?"

I thought for a moment. I really did want to be like my big friends and I nodded my head. Mama kissed me on the cheek and she walked me back to the kindergarten room. "Now you skeedaddle," she said and lightly slapped me on my bottom. I slowly walked toward the door. If Luey, John, and David could do it, then I could too. I stepped into the room and never looked back.

The month of May arrived and Benny Sawyer, a little freckle-faced boy with bright red hair, sat next to me on our front porch. He was a year older than me, but I had still beat him in a rock fight just moments before. He lightly touched the bump on his forehead where I had bounced a good size rock off it. "Boy, you sure can throw," he said as he felt the bump.

"Yeah, I know. I practice a lot," I said proudly. "I hit my mama in the

side of the head last week with a rock, and she sure whipped the fire out
of me."

"Oh, I'd never hit my mama with a rock," Benny said.

"It was a mistake. I thought it was my sister. I just heard the heavy
footsteps on the porch steps and I figured it was Linda, so I jumped out
quick as a cat from around the side of the house and pitched it as hard as I
could toward the front steps without even looking. The next thing I know,
Mama dropped her groceries and she's bent over holding her head."

"Did you tell her it was a mistake?"

"Nope."

"How come?"

"When she stopped rubbing her head she looked up at me. Her eyes
were all bugged out, she gnashed her teeth and started saying things that I
had never heard before, then here she comes running right for me."

"Whadja do?"

"I ran! I had her beat too, except I made the mistake of stopping by the
back door and peeking around the corner to see if she had gone around the
house. The next thing I know I hear the screen-door spring creak. I was
just getting ready to run when this long arm comes out the back door and
grabs me by the back of the neck."

"She whipped you good, huh?"

"Yep, sure wish it had been Linda," I said.

Benny nodded his head in agreement. "Your mama is about the prettiest mama in the whole world. Look! Here she comes now."

I was proud when I looked up the street as Mama came home from
work. She was pretty. She had pretty brown eyes and red lips, and curly
brown hair, and she was fair-skinned.

She smiled and greeted us as we sat on the porch.

"Hi, baby, hi Benny," she said and walked into the house.

"And she smells the prettiest too," Benny said as the scent of her perfume reached our noses. "She smells better than doughnuts," Benny
added. I nodded in agreement, but I didn't know what doughnuts were.
Later that night I heard Mama and Dad talking. Dad said that he wanted
me to go to "catty-chism," and I kind of liked the idea because I liked
cats. Sunday came and Linda and I walked to the little church called Guadalupe. There was a whole bunch of other Mexican kids there, and soon a
nun came out and talked to the older children. I was still looking for cats
as we were ushered into a small room with long benches that had high

backs. Sister Mary Margaret stood before us. She talked real loud, but I didn't pay any attention. I just knew those cats were in there somewhere and I was ready to get my hands on one. The next thing I knew she was talking in a language that I had never heard before. All at once the other children dropped to their knees, and I alone stood until Linda grabbed me by the arm and pulled me down. But that didn't stop Sister Mary Margaret. She looked hard at me, then slowly she walked over and from out of nowhere produced a long stick that I found out later they called a ruler. Whack! I didn't have time to duck before she popped me on the head with the stick. I grabbed my head with both hands and looked to my sister for protection. Linda just smiled at me.

"Pay attention, little boy, and do as the other children do or I will have to correct you again." Sister Mary Margaret started to walk away. "Where are the cats?" I asked. All the children laughed aloud. She paused for a moment, then turned and glared at me.

"There are no cats in the house of God," she said loudly.

"My daddy said I was going to catty-chism, but there aren't any cats here." All the children laughed uncontrollably as the Sister made a bee-line for me. She grabbed me hard by the shoulder and shook me.

"Now you listen, little boy, you better straighten up or I'm going to wear your britches out." All was quiet in the room as she pushed me down on my knees. I looked up at Linda, who was still smiling. "I wanna go home," I said.

"Ssshh, just be quiet and do like the other kids. You'll be okay."

That was my first and last experience with catechism. I went to church picnics and parties but I stayed clear of Sister Mary Margaret. From that day on I always carried a rock with me, just in case.

That night Linda told Mama about me and Sister Mary Margaret, and Linda was laughing about it, while Mama tried not to smile. "Poor baby," she said, and she looked at me with a sorry expression.

"Mama, I want to go to church with you, and be what you are."

Of course I didn't know it then, but Mama was eating that up.

"You can go with me Sunday," she said smiling. "Grandpa would love to have you in his church."

I looked at Linda and stuck my tongue out at her, and she acted like she had a ruler in her hand, and she swatted the invisible ruler at my head, and I yelled for Mama as Linda giggled.

I heard Mama and Daddy talking one night, and Mama took up for me cause I didn't know Latin, the language that Sister Mary Margaret had used at catechism. Heck, I didn't even know Spanish, and I was a little Mexican boy. I asked Mama if there were any Sisters at Grandpa's church and she assured me that there were none. Yep, ol' Sister Mary Margaret would have to find another head to bop, and I hoped it would be little Tino Casilla's, who always managed to steal my Hostess Snowballs at the church picnics.

Sunday morning arrived, and Mama and Daddy and I drove to Okmulgee, Oklahoma, where my grandpa, Newman McIntosh, was the Baptist preacher. "Preacher" was what Grandma Annie had called Grandpa for as long as I could remember. He was almost full-blood Creek, except for the little bit of Scots in him, and Grandma was full-blood Creek. Grandpa was tall, with what they called salt-and-pepper hair. He had gray eyes and wore reading glasses. Grandma was real short and round, and her hair was always fastened up with a barrette. Her eyes were almond shaped, kind of like a Chinese lady's; she was my grandma and I loved her. I was dressed in my favorite cowboy suit. It was a thick black shirt with red fringe down the arms, black pants, and black cowboy boots. Best of all, I had a red bandanna around my neck. I smiled as I walked with Mama and Daddy into the small white church just west of Okmulgee. All the men sat on the left side of the church, and all the women sat on the right. So Daddy walked over to the left side and sat next to a little gray-haired Indian man. I followed Mama to the right side and Mama sat next to a big old fat Indian woman, who smiled and said something in Creek to Mama. Mama told her I was five years old, and the woman smiled again as she looked at me.

I was proud that my grandpa was the preacher here. I would be a good little boy, and be saved, and know what the heck was being said to me, and I wouldn't even have to get down on my knees. HALLELUJAH! As I sat next to my mother on the hard, unpainted bench, I felt safe and content. I looked around the room at the fat old ladies. Some of them wore the wildest-looking hats I had ever seen. One lady had a net over her face, and I knew that was to keep the flies from getting in her mouth. Another lady had a big old orange feather sticking up from her leopard-skin hat, and another woman looked like someone had stuck a plant on her head. But they thought they were "gussied up," that's what Mama always called it. The men wore clean white shirts and dark pants, a few old men just wore bib overalls with clean shirts, and boots. Suddenly I felt pain, real pain on the top of my head. I grabbed my head with both hands and turned to see what had fallen on me. There before me was a dark, wrinkled old Indian man with bushy, snow-white hair. He wore black pants, dirty worn cowboy boots, and a clean white shirt. In his hand he held a cane. He shook the cane at me and motioned for me to look straight ahead. I looked up at Mama, and she was smiling at me. And I couldn't figure out why, every time I got thumped on the head, everybody always smiled. I didn't think it was the least bit funny.

"Deacon Harjo wants you to sit up and pay attention," Mama said, patting me on the knee.

Deacons! Oh God, this place had deacons with clubs. I turned and looked at Deacon Harjo, who stood no more than six feet away. He was looking straight at me. We made eye contact. He raised his cane and took a step toward me. As quick as I could, I turned around and looked straight ahead. I waited for the pain to start. Just then Grandpa entered the pulpit. He wore navy slacks with a white shirt opened at the collar. On his feet he wore freshly polished, black lace-up shoes. In his right hand he held a worn black Bible. He raised his hands to the congregation and said in a loud voice, "Mado." Time out! Yep, you guessed it. The entire sermon was spoken in the Creek language. I was doomed to be a sinner!

The month of June arrived and the neighborhood buzzed with activity. Kids were everywhere. Me, I was busy climbing peach trees for Mr. Archueleta. Mr. Archueleta had six peach trees in his backyard, and he and I had a deal. If I climbed the trees and filled his basket with peaches, he would let me eat all I could of them and he would even peel them for me. We even shook on it. I knew I was growing up, because I had my first job already. Rose, his daughter, held the basket for me. I climbed the first tree, its sap was gooey and icky to my skin as I climbed from one limb to the next. I picked the peaches and dropped them in the basket that Rose held. Rose was eight years old. Afterward we sat on her back porch eating the fresh peaches, and she asked if I wanted to go into her daddy's garage. I said sure. We stepped inside through double doors. The garage was old and unpainted. You could see daylight through the slats of board that were nailed up to the frame. Rays of sunlight filtered through the cracks, and I watched the dust particles become visible in the sunlight. Suddenly, Rose spoke.

"Hey, Vincent, do you wanna kiss?"

"Kiss, what?"

"Me! That's what boys and girls do!"

"Why?"

"Because they're supposed to."

I thought a moment, "Naw, I only kiss my mama," I said. She stepped toward me. She was eight and I was five and she was a good head taller than me, and I stepped back as she approached me. I kept backing up until I backed into the wall of the garage. I was trapped. A stack of old tires was on my left and a huge stack of boxes on my right. I looked up into Rose's dark face. She wasn't pretty and she wasn't ugly, she was just a girl. A big girl.

"C'mon, just a little kiss is all I want."

"Nope! I don't wanna kiss you," I said and I wondered what my hero Wild Bill Hickok would do in this predicament. Suddenly she grabbed me by my throat with her left hand and drew back her right fist. It got bigger and bigger as I looked at it. Her right hand waved in the air full of power, full of knuckles . . . big knuckles.

"You better kiss me or I'm gonna poke you right in the nose!" she said through clenched teeth.

I wiggled to get free, but years of scratching her head had developed her grip, and I gave in to her terms.

"Okay! Okay, I'll kiss you!" I blurted out, and she smiled and relaxed her grip on my throat.

"Now here's how you do it," she instructed. "You pucker your lips like this," and she puckered her mouth like she had just sucked on a lemon. "Then you close your eyes and kiss."

It sounded easy enough, but I still couldn't figure out why. She made me practice once without her and then I heard her say "Perfect!"

"Okay, on the count of one, you pucker. On the count of two, you close your eyes. And on three, I'm gonna kiss you." Her eyes danced as she spoke. She counted one and I puckered, she counted two and I closed my eyes, she counted three and I felt her big peach-eating lips on mine . . . yuck! She kissed me for about three seconds but it seemed like three hours, and as she pulled away from me she was all smiles.

"Wasn't that wonderful, Vincent?" she said.

I wiped my lips across my forearm and then spit on the dirt floor. She put her hands on her hips and looked at me in disgust.

"Hmph! You just don't know what's fun," and she turned and quickly walked out the garage door. I wiped my mouth again and spit one more time for good measure. I slowly walked outside, took a few steps, and then turned to look back at the open garage doors. "I ain't going back in there," I said to myself, and then I heard Mama calling for me and I lit out for our front porch at a dead run.

TWO // **Little Boy of Color**

The days were getting hot, and Junior and the Bargas boys were going to Newblock Park to swim. It was for big boys only, that's what Luey Bargas told me. He was great big, with black curly hair, and he went to high school. I figured they called it high school cause everybody was tall that went there. Luey said that they had to walk all the way across town to get to Newblock and that I was too little to go. My swimming hole was the curb. I had to wait for a rainstorm, and then Benny Sawyer and I would lie down in the street next to the curb and let the water run over us. We were happy, and we didn't even have to walk across town.

That was the summer I learned to ride a bicycle. That was a sight. Daddy bought me a red bicycle at an auction. It was just my size. Daddy would hold on to the bike as I peddled down the driveway and then he'd let go and I'd fall over and crash. I'd cry for a while and then get back on and we'd do it all over again. Mama mentioned something called training wheels, but Daddy said they cost money and he didn't have any, so I continued to crash and cry. One day I came home from visiting the Cervantes family that lived just up the street from us. Daddy was putting on some little wheels on the back of my bicycle. He sat me on my bike and I took off. A week later the training wheels came off, and I knew for a fact that I was on my way to becoming a big boy.

One evening Benny and I were playing marbles in the backyard, when suddenly we heard Rose and Junior scream in the front yard. In an instant children and adults converged on our front yard as Rose cried and Junior was wide-eyed with terror. He put one finger on each side of his head like horns, made a sign about his chin, and pointed up in the tree that stood in our front yard. Just then Rose was able to talk. It was the devil, she screamed, and they had both seen him perched among the tree limbs. The Mexican men and women talked to each other in Spanish as Sonya led Rose home and Mama took Junior in the house. That night I heard Mama and Daddy talking and Daddy told Mama that Mr. Archueleta had heard of such a tale in his hometown of Piedras Negras, in Mexico, and that it had been the work of a "bruja," a witch, and that Daddy should keep an eye on us kids.

That night I sat on the floor close to Mama as she sewed on her sewing machine. We listened to the radio and I laughed at *The Great Gildersleeve* and *Amos and Andy.* Things got spooky as we listened to *The Shadow,* and the scariest of all was *Inner Sanctum.* As I heard the creaking door open on the radio, I was in an instant beneath Mama's sewing machine and I had a death grip on her legs. She had to stop sewing and pry my hands loose. Just then a police bulletin came over the radio, and it said there were prowlers in the area of North Utica and Independence. "That's our neighborhood," I heard Linda say, but Mama said not to worry. When Linda and I crawled into bed together I asked her what prowlers were, and she said they were great big hairy creatures with red eyes and long teeth that came out at night and loved to eat the flesh of little boys; then she smiled real big and rolled over. She didn't have anything to worry about because she was just a girl. I stayed awake most of the night watching for prowlers, but none ever showed up, and I breathed a sigh of relief when I saw the sun shining the next morning.

This was my very first experience with the spirit world. The word "bruja" stayed in my mind. I would soon learn about shamans and witches. In fact my own great-grandfather, Temiye Kernels, was a Creek medicine man. He blew smoke and was one with the invisible world. This was part of the Mexican and Indian world, and I accepted it for fact. I accepted it because I had been told by my parents, but years later I would see with my own eyes the power of the invisible world, a world that is very real. The white world has its God and skeptics, the Indians have their Great Spirit but few if any skeptics when it comes to "medicine," for we of the Indian race have seen the power of the "medicine." Even though the way of the Great Spirit has been taken from us and Christianity taught to us, we still believe in "medicine." The Mexicans have their Catholic Church, and a few belong to other denominations, but even though they believe in God and his teachings, they still talk of brujos and brujas.

We moved to North Quincy Street before the summer was out. Uncle Claude had bought the property. There was a three-room house at the front of the property and a one-room house located behind it. We lived in the three-room house, while Uncle Frank and my Grandma Mendoza lived in the one-room house. We called Frank "Uncle Pancho," and we called Grandma "Waleeta" because Daddy didn't think we could pronounce "Abuelita," which means "Little Grandma." She was under five feet tall and her long gray hair would fall to her waist whenever she took it loose. She looked after me when I came home from school. She spoke not a word of English; the closest she could come was "hamboogie," which was a hamburger. I learned three words: "sentarse," "callarse," and "comer." Sit down, shut up, and eat. What else does a six-year-old need to know? Uncle Pancho spoke Spanish and English, like Dad, Claude, and my Aunt Connie. The white kids would taunt us at school, and call us names like "stupid Mexicans," but I figured we weren't stupid because my Dad could speak two languages and I bet their dads couldn't.

When I came home from school, Waleeta would make me some tortillas. I would sit on the floor and watch her as her busy hands rolled out the wonderful bread. Then she would flop the dough onto a small round skillet and cook the tortilla, first on one side then the other. She also made chile (salsa) from fresh ground peppers that Uncle Poncho would bring home from the Trenton Market. The best part would be when she smeared butter on the hot tortilla and I would crawl under her work table and she would hand it to me, and as fast as she could make them I would devour them.

Of course I had a job that I had to do, and I hated it. It was my job to empty Waleeta's pee pot. Oh, how I hated to do that. It was heavy and smelly. Sometimes it was filled to the brim, and I would have to take it out to the outhouse and pour it down the plumbed toilet, all the while holding my breath and trying not to spill any on me.

I got into a lot of trouble at school during the first grade and the principal and I were on a first-name basis . . . at least he was. One day I forgot my coat and hurried back to Mrs. Schaeffer's room to get it. While I was in the cloakroom I heard Mrs. Schaeffer talking to Mr. Brann, the principal.

"Which class should I fail?" she asked.

"I don't know and I don't care. All I know is that we're overcrowded, and you have to fail one of your two classes. There's just no room for them all in the second grade."

"It's not fair to them, Howard."

"I know, but we've got to do it."

"Well, I'm not going to fail my homeroom."

"Well, then, there you have it. You do what you have to do, but you will do it." Then he turned and stormed out of the room. I hid behind a coat, so he didn't see me as he walked out. Mrs. Schaeffer was looking down at her desk and shaking her head. And as luck would have it, I was not in her homeroom class. I tried to explain it to Mama and Daddy, but they wouldn't listen. Daddy scolded me for getting in trouble, and Mama hurt me worse by saying she was disappointed in me. I got mad and asked them, "If I'm the cause of it, why did my entire class fail?" Ha! I had them, in my six-year-old logic. But their minds were made up and the next year when school started they had their hands full. Mr. Brann and I saw each other every day. Then one day Mama and I had to go see Mr. Brann. That's when I told them that I had heard Mr. Brann tell Mrs. Schaeffer to fail my class, and I wanted Mr. Brann to confess what he had done. He didn't do it, and he blamed it all on me. He said I was immature and I told him maybe I was, but at least I wasn't a liar. Mama got mad at me for saying it. When we got home she mentioned something about politics, and that I was to make the best of a done deal. I didn't know it then, but that's what had happened to the Indians a hundred years before. We would always have to make the best of a done deal.

One night a week my Aunt Connie and Uncle Joe Perez would come over to the house and watch *I Love Lucy*, on our television. I liked for them to come over. Mama would fix coffee, and they'd all laugh at Lucy, and when Desi ranted and raved in Spanish, they would really laugh. It was at this time in my life that I became interested in playing music. Dad bought me a pair of maracas and a set of claves. Claves are two wooden sticks that are struck together to make a loud clicking sound, and maracas are round gourds filled with beads that make a noise like a baby rattle. Dad had some records by Xavier Cugat, and a Mexican group called "The Trio los Panchos," and I would stand and play with them for hours, Mama would always have to call me to the supper table, and Daddy would always rub my head when I came running.

We moved to the west side of Tulsa during my third-grade year. I was the lookout for some older boys who were always getting in trouble in the old neighborhood, and I don't know if that had anything to do with the move, but I hated leaving North Quincy. I remember when I first saw the house on West Brady Street. It looked like a mansion to me. The back porch was enclosed and I liked that. Daddy opened the back door and the first room we came to was a breakfast room. Then we entered the kitchen, and I just stood with my mouth open and looked about at all the cabinets and the space. I walked into the dining room and looked at the carpet on the floor. We never had carpet before. My Uncle Claude had carpet in his living room, and until now that was the only carpet I had ever seen. The carpet extended into the living room, which seemed huge to me. This was more than I could have ever imagined. I stood in the middle of the dining room and turned in a slow circle, looking at all the empty space. Dad called to me from across a hallway and I walked over to him. He was standing in the bathroom. My mouth dropped open. It had a toilet and a sink, it even had a huge bathtub. "Daddy, let's get this house," I said, as I remembered the bitter cold winter nights, and the rain. No more getting fully dressed in the middle of the night. Then Daddy showed us the three bedrooms, and of course Linda had to have her own bedroom. I just didn't know why God made sisters, all they did was make trouble. Daddy showed me the back bedroom that I would share with Junior and that was okay, because Junior was away at his school most of the time. The house also had an attic fan, a floor furnace, and a thing called a hot water tank. No more heating water on the stove for this guy, I thought as I looked about the mansion. The icing on the cake was the two-car garage. It was huge, and it had a workshop in the back. Now Dad had a place of his own, but he said he was going to buy a Ping-Pong table and put it in the shop. We all cheered, then I asked what a Ping-Pong table was, and Linda said her favorite phrase, "You're so stupid." I got her back real good by saying, "At least I don't have hairy legs, like a monkey," and she tried to hit me, but I was too fast. I knew that Daddy wouldn't allow her to shave her legs. If I caught her in just the right mood I could make her cry by making sounds like a monkey . . . it was great. I thought I was the richest kid in the world. I asked Mama and Daddy if we were going to have a maid, and they just laughed.

Mom enrolled me at Pershing Elementary School. She took me to my first class, then left for work. I met Mrs. Downing and took my place at an empty desk. As I looked around all the kids were giving me dirty looks. I ate lunch by myself. What's their problem, I thought, I hadn't done anything to them, why heck, I didn't even know them, and they were all making stupid faces at me, and talking to each other while looking at me. I walked out of the lunchroom and noticed a group of boys watching me.

They all stopped talking when they saw me and the biggest boy of the group walked over to me.

"Why don't you go back where you came from, nigger," he said as the other boys surrounded me. "Yeah, China man, go home," taunted another boy. "He's a dirty Jap, that's what he is," another added.

"I ain't no Jap, I'm Mexican-Indian," I said, standing my ground, fist clenched. I was the only dark-skinned person in the entire school.

"Yuck, that's worse, you're a greaser," the big boy said.

"Yeah, he's a dirty Injun."

Just then I heard a woman's voice from behind me.

"You boys get out of here and leave him alone." I watched their faces as they all looked at the lady behind me and then quickly scattered, saying nothing.

I turned and looked up at the lady. She was tall with gray hair, she wore glasses, and she was smiling at me. And best of all she was Indian! She bent forward resting her hands on her knees.

"Looks like you and me are the only Indians in this big city school," she said smiling.

"Yes, ma'am," I paused for a moment, "I'm part Mexican too," I said. "My name's Vincent Mendoza," and I stuck my hand out to shake her hand.

"My name is Mrs. Root, I'm the school librarian," and she pointed into the lunchroom. "Do you see all those books in there?"

"Yes, ma'am."

"Well, you can read any of them that you want to. I'll fix you up a library card when I see you this afternoon," she said still smiling.

I thanked her and headed for the door to the playground. I stopped and turned around to look at her and she was still standing there watching. I waved at her and she waved back, then I stepped out into the sunlight.

I overcame the racism by picking a fight with the toughest guy in our class. He was twelve years old and still in the third grade. I got the tar kicked out of me but gained his respect by giving him a bloody nose. I also gained the respect of the other kids, and soon was asked to play baseball with the third-grade team. That spring I became a Pershing Bobcat, and I would develop a lifetime love for baseball. One team we played was Riley Elementary. As we piled out of the coach's car to get warmed up by throwing the ball around, one of the white kids started yelling, "Hey look

they got a nigger on their team! Hey look, it's a nigger!'' I just smiled at
him, and he smiled back.

"Who are you?'' he asked. "Minnie Minoso?''

"Nope. Call me Jackie.''

"Jackie who?''

"Jackie Robinson, stupid.'' We won the ball game 10 to 1.

By the time I was in the fourth grade Dad had taught me how to play
the saxophone. I wanted to play the guitar, and so Dad being Dad, I
learned to play the sax. I hated practicing. I'd fuss and cry and he'd yell at
me, and threaten to lock me in my room, but I had him there, because we
didn't have any locks on the doors. Anyway, it was a daily ritual, and I
would practice for an hour and then be free for the rest of the evening.
Dad had bought me a secondhand C melody saxophone, its pitch was
in between a tenor and alto sax. Dad was "King of the Second Hand
Stores," and he was proud of his ability to find a real bargain. I didn't
know it then, but I'd be on the receiving end of "Real Bargains" until I
left home. Meanwhile Linda was watching *American Bandstand*, it was
sickening to hear her squeal whenever she saw a cute guy.

The only thing I really hated was practicing baseball with my dad.
He'd get mad and cuss whenever I'd miss a ground ball or misjudge a fly
ball. I'd be in tears and he would continue to throw too hard and my left
hand would be black and blue with bruises. I could play ball, but whenever Dad showed up at the game I'd be so scared that I just couldn't do
anything at all. I loved baseball with the guys, but I was beginning to hate
my dad. I remember one game when I struck out with the bases loaded. I
was the last out of the game, and Dad cussed me out all the way home.
The next day was a Saturday and he took me back to the ball diamond for
batting practice. He kept hitting me with the pitches, then he'd cuss me
some more. Finally, I'd had enough, and as he hit me square in the back
with a pitch I turned and threw the bat at him as hard as I could, barely
missing his head. He threw down his glove and rushed me and I didn't
move. I glared at him as he slapped me with his open palm, again and
again he hit me across the back and shoulders, and I never let out a whim-
per, I just glared at him. He finally stopped when he saw that he couldn't
make me cry. That was the last time we ever practiced baseball together.
When I grew older Mom told me of Dad's passion for baseball. He had
played baseball all his life and when we lived in the Mexican neighborhood he worked for Lee C. Moore as a sheetmetal layout man. The com-

pany had a baseball team in the industrial league and Dad had been an all-star shortstop for five consecutive years until he was injured in a game. He expected perfection because he had been perfection in his own eye . . . but not in mine.

By the time I was in the fifth grade I could read and play any kind of sheet music that was put in front of me. Anything at all. Mom and Dad were pretty proud of me. He let Linda and me play a duet in front of my Uncle Claude and Charlie, and we raised their eyebrows. Linda played baritone sax at Central High. She only played it to meet boys. Dad taught me how to play the piano and read piano music, and I got pretty good at it. So good in fact that Dad invited Charlie's daughter, Rosalie, to play with Linda and me. Rosalie played the clarinet, or let's say she tried to play the clarinet. We sounded like a bunch of trained seals and Dad grabbed his head again, while Charlie just laughed and shook his head. Dad was a perfectionist. Whether it was music or playing ball, if it wasn't done correctly then he was ranting and raving . . . he did a lot of both.

It was the summer of my eleventh year, and as we drove to see my Grandma and Grandpa McIntosh I grew eager. I always had fun and adventure at their home. My cousins Butch, Brenda, and Charley LaSarge were always there, along with William, Pug, Shirley, Vickie, and baby Marilyn McIntosh. We had fun listening to the people at church sing in the Creek language. We only picked up the bad words and the phrase, "hum bucs che," which means, "when do we eat?" Grandma and Grandpa spoke Creek to each other and the other Creeks, but they never attempted to teach us the language. We were satisfied with just the juicy parts and I don't think that we could have made up a sentence between all of us. The Okmulgee Indian Baptist Church was located west of the city of Okmulgee. There were maybe half a dozen houses there, along with the little white church and a large brush arbor (an open-air meeting place made of poles holding up a brushwood roof). They had electricity, but no running water or gas. Grandma still cooked on her wood-burning stove, and we had to fill large milk cans full of water at the water department downtown.

For years we had talked with an old Indian man who lived in one of the camp houses. His name was Joseph Smoke. He told us stories. Some were scary, and some were not. This was my first trip to my grandparents in quite a while and we played hard all day. After supper when we ran outside to play as always, Grandma turned on the back porch light for us. It had just gotten dark, the last rays of the sun were orange on the horizon. We were playing tag and I ran to the edge of the light; for an instant I looked toward the road that circled the graveyard and passed by Grandpa's garage, about forty feet from the back door. I recognized the stooped shoulders and the slow shuffle of Joseph Smoke. I called out to him and waved. He stopped on the road in the fading light and just stared at me. I started to run to him when suddenly my cousin Butch tackled me, knocking me to the ground. The other children scattered in all directions, running and screaming, as I fought to get loose from Butch.

"Let me go, Butch! Let's go see Joseph, he's standing right over there," I said. Butch was wide-eyed, and for an instant he couldn't speak. Then he blurted out, "Joseph Smoke died two weeks ago!" We stared at each other eyeball to eyeball, then turned to look at Joseph Smoke. He was still standing there watching us as we ran screaming into the house. The adults paid us no mind and continued their conversation. All of us children sat quietly in the middle of the living room.

This was the first time I had ever seen a spirit. My cousins had seen the spirit too, and now as I reflect on the happening I realize that maybe Great-Grandfather Temiye Kernels had given each of us a gift, or perhaps it was just the love that Joseph Smoke felt for each of us that carried over with him into the invisible world.

I loved to spend weekends at Grandma's. They still slept on feather beds at their house, I would lie there and feel the mattress engulf me, it was a marvelous feeling. In the morning a rooster would crow, and I could hear hens clucking and scratching outside my window. I would lie there and smell the delicious aroma of bacon, and coffee, and I knew Grandma and Mama were up fixing breakfast. I would rise and dress, then walk to the back porch to wash up for breakfast. Breakfast at Grandma's was something special to me. Stacks of biscuits, bacon piled high, jelly and butter. Eggs fresh from the nest and cooked to perfection. What more could a boy want? Soon my cousins would return and we would be off on an adventure. Sometimes we would lie in the tall grass twenty yards or so behind the women's outhouse, waiting for Grandma or some other elderly woman to go inside. We would give her time to get seated, then we would throw a barrage of dirt clods up on the wooden walls and tin roof. Fluent Creek would erupt from the out-house and we would laugh heartily. Soon the occupant would walk outside and shake her dress out, then be on her way, all the while mumbling in Creek. Other times we would harass a sow who'd just had piglets. Being young and mostly stupid we never realized the danger when we took turns jumping into the pen, picking up a stray piglet, and running with it to the rail fence as the three- to four-hundred-pound sow charged us. We would drop the piglet just before we leaped over the fence. The huge sow would slam into the rails and we would laugh as she grunted and chomped her teeth at us. We'd wait for her to get settled down, then we'd do it again.

Of course we played the traditional kid games like red rover, tag, hide-and-seek, and football and baseball. And when you had ten to fifteen kids, counting the neighbors' kids, you could have a lot of fun. We never had a real ball, the football would be a wad of newspapers taped up. Of course if you had a football game, you'd have a zillion "dog piles" on someone; there's nothing quite like running with abandon and jumping as high as you can and landing on some poor soul who's out of breath, and whose eyes are protruding from his skull. Ah, sweet youth. Moronic behavior was acceptable; this is part of being a kid—although it is sometimes carried over into the adult world, as exemplified by our government and judicial system, but that's another story.

These were the happy days of my youth. I could only wish that someday I too would live on a farm and be awakened every morning by a rooster greeting the dawn of a new day; in that instant I would be transported back in time . . . Grandma and Grandpa would still be alive, and I and my cousins would still be little and crazy. Every morning as the cock crowed, what a stirring within, what a remembrance of days gone by. I could ask for no greater a gift than a cock crowing at the dawn.

School resumed in September. I enjoyed my teachers at Pershing Elementary, with the exception of Mrs. Soward, my speech teacher. We were rehearsing a Thanksgiving play and of course I was chosen as the Indian chief. I stood proudly on stage. One of the little girls in my class stood next to me. She was playing the part of a pilgrim. Mrs. Soward had a fit when she saw the girl standing next to me. She shrieked and pulled the girl away. "Never, ever, stand next to an Indian," she said. "They never take baths, they go to the bathroom in the woods. They wear stinking animal skins, oh my, never stand next to an Indian, dear. Remember, you're a pilgrim, and he's a dirty, stinking Indian!" All the children stepped away from me like I had the plague. She really did hurt my feelings. I decided that she was just a silly old white woman.

My favorite teacher was Miss Coughlin, my music teacher. She was tall, she had dark brown hair, she wore glasses, and she was beautiful. I just knew that I'd grow up and return to Pershing and marry her just like that. One day she let us sing solos in front of the class. One kid sang "Round and Round" like Perry Como, then another boy sang "Sixteen Tons" like Tennessee Ernie Ford, and then I raised my hand. Miss Coughlin called on me and I slowly walked to the front of the class, with all eyes focused on me. I stuck one hand in the air and cut loose with the first verse . . . "You ain't nothin' but a hound dog!" The place went wild! I shook everything I could, just like Elvis, as the girls screamed and Miss Coughlin laughed till she cried. Elvis didn't have a thing on this kid. From that day on I was a hit with the girls, and most of all Miss Coughlin.

As I entered the fourth grade we were awakened to a new interest, Cub Scouts. Mrs. Oliver was our den mother. How she put up with us I'll never know. We looked so cool with our little blue caps and blue shirts with yellow neckerchiefs, yep, nothing like a boy in uniform to make those girls look twice. Of course I liked the uniform because it was the closest thing to a cavalry uniform that I could get my hands on. I was a western buff! I loved those blue uniforms and big black boots, and the thought of carrying a saber and riding a horse, shooting a six-shooter . . . my God, what more could a boy want, or ever need! I never thought about the Indians, I felt like a traitor . . . well, not really. Indians just weren't flashy enough. Loin cloths and a single feather, riding a spotted pony . . . naw, give me the saber! I did manage to find a happy medium, the Apache scouts. They wore blue coats, and they were cool looking. If you were going to be part of the Old West you had to look cool. Roy, Hopalong, Lash La Rue, Gene, Tex, they were all cool, even Gabby.

During our fifth-grade year we moved up to Webelos, the top dogs of Cub Scoutdom, and next year we would be able to become Boy Scouts! This was also the year that I would become a professional entertainer. Dad and the band were playing a dance at the local Veterans of Foreign Wars post on Sixth Street near downtown Tulsa. The band was onstage, and Ray, Claude's oldest son, had joined the group as a maraca player; he also played guitar and sang. I was just offstage behind some curtains, and I saw a set of bongo drums that Ray had brought along. As the Mendoza family played a cha-cha, I picked up the drums and started playing along.

As soon as the song ended I turned around and looked into the faces of the entire band. "I won't do it again," I said. Uncle Claude laughed. "No, no, Banson," he couldn't say Vincent, "you are good, you keep playing those bongos!" The rest of the band including Dad were all smiles. They invited me out onstage, but I declined. I was content to play my first dance behind the curtains. The next practice Uncle Claude asked me to join the band. I was so proud I could have burst! I was the newest member of "Claude Mendoza and His Mariachis."

A week later I saw a moving van stop just around the corner from my house. Being nosy and with nothing better to do I casually walked over to the corner of Waco and Brady. A new family was moving in. I saw a little boy carrying a pillow, then another boy, then two more appeared from around the front of the truck. The two older boys saw me and one of them waved and yelled to me, "Hey, Chief!" Who in the heck is that, I thought, and I waved, then slowly walked toward the two boys. An older man and a pretty lady walked past them and into the house. I still didn't recognize the short-haired boy smiling at me.

"Do I know you?" I asked.

He laughed and elbowed his brother, "Hey, George, he don't recognize me." Both boys laughed. "Stand like you're going to hit a baseball," he instructed. I stood with arms raised holding my invisible bat. He squatted down like a catcher, just off to one side, then he looked up at me. "You can't hit this guy," he said. It was "Wise Guy"! I recognized the phrase and his voice. He was a catcher for the Mark Twain Elementary School's baseball team. We had played against each other for over two years now, but all I had ever seen as I looked into the catcher's mask was a pair of eyes, a mass of freckles, and a couple of teeth hanging out. "You can't hit this guy" was his favorite phrase, and the first time he said it I had answered, "Watch this, wise guy," and promptly smashed a double. Every time I'd cross home plate he'd playfully swing at me with his glove. He always wore his catcher's mask. He was small for his age, with brown hair cut real short. His face was covered with freckles and he had a friendly smile. He stuck out his hand to shake and introduced himself. "My name's Arnold Horner," he said smiling as we shook hands. "This here is my brother George," then George and I shook hands as Arnold's two little brothers came outside. "The ugly one there is Johnny," Arnold said. "Which one is that?" I asked, and all the brothers laughed. "I'm Jackie," the littlest one said. "He's the ugly one," and he pointed at his brother Johnny. Johnny was freckle-faced and wore glasses. He waved at me, then he and Jackie hurried out to the van.

Arnold and I became the best of friends. The summer before we entered the seventh grade, Arnold and I walked the few blocks to Newblock Park. Soon we were swimming and splashing in the cool, clear water of the city-operated pool. We were sitting in the water on the ropes that divided the deep end of the pool from the shallow end when suddenly I heard my name being called. I turned and couldn't believe my eyes. It was Glenda Miles! She was two years older than I, with long brown curly hair, blue eyes, and a budding beautiful body. Next to her stood her little friend Hilda Tate. I heard Glenda call my name again and then she waved. I immediately swam toward her. What would Glenda Miles want to talk to me about?

"Hi, Vince!"

"Hi, Glenda, hi, Hilly," I said, not even looking at Hilda. My eyes danced as I looked upon the beauty of Glenda Miles.

"Vince, you like me don't you?"

"Sure, you bet, Glenda."

"Well, we, uh, I was wondering if you would like to * $ # @."

"What?" I had no idea what she was talking about.

She rolled her eyes, "You know, * $ # @."

I thought frantically . . . what could that be? "Hold on, I'll be right back." I half-swam half-ran to Arnold who was still sitting on the ropes. "Hey, Arnie, what's * $ # @ ?"

"I don't know, why?"

"Well, Glenda Miles wants to know if I want to * $ # @."

We both thought. Our little brains had never heard that word. Arnold broke the silence, "Ya better tell her no, cause you might get into trouble." Hey, that was good enough for me, I certainly didn't know what else to say. I swam back to Glenda. She and Hilda were giggling and all smiles as I approached them.

"Weeell," said Glenda smiling.

"No thanks, not today."

Glenda's mouth flew open and she and Hilda looked at each other in disbelief. "Oh, you, you, you boy!" Glenda yelled. Hilda looked at me and added, "Yeah!" They both turned and stormed away. What did I say?

Two weeks later Arnold and I were at the ball diamond, and I asked two older boys what * $ # @ was. Arnold and I stood with our mouths open as they explained. A light bulb came on in my brain. I turned and looked angrily down at Arnold. He looked up at me and smiled; suddenly he took off at a dead run toward center field. I was hot on his heels . . . "AAARRRNNOOLLDDD!!!!"

THREE // **My Stupid Years**

September 1960 was the beginning of my stupid years. The stupid years would continue throughout my life, but this was the beginning. Seventh grade beckoned and Arnold and I met each other at the corner of Waco and Brady on a bright Monday morning. We each wore new blue jeans and tennis shoes—black high-top Keds—and a new shirt. In our arms we carried new notebooks, paper, and pencils. Ha! Bring on that old seventh grade, you teachers will earn your pay this year, that's for sure! We slowly walked up the street toward Roosevelt Junior High School, muttering "I hate school" every other step of the half-mile down West Easton Street toward the looming three-story brick structure at the intersection of Quanah and West Easton. As we stood at that intersection waiting for traffic to clear I was filled with dread. Why hadn't I been born a hundred years before? I'd be riding a pony somewhere in the woods, or hunting the wily deer, or even better yet, scouting for a war party. But no, not me, I was standing on the corner with Arnold waiting for the traffic to clear. As we stepped off the curb, we spoke at the same time and said the same words, "I hate school!"

It turned out school really wasn't that bad and the new faces were refreshing, new people, new challenges, new ideas, new feelings. Feelings? I was a seventh grader, a Boy Scout for pete's sake, what new feelings could I ever experience? . . . This is where the stupid part starts.

I was sitting in Mrs. Batchelor's English class listening to her read *Evangeline*. She was short, plump, bespectacled, and I was sure that she was someone's sweet grandmother. So with my elbow on my desk and my chin resting on my hand I listened silently with the other bored-stiff students. Out of the corner of my eye I could see someone watching me. I turned to look at the girl, and she quickly looked away. I didn't think anything about it, but when I looked away she turned to look at me again. We did this a couple of times. Finally I quit looking at her, and she continued to stare. Suddenly it struck me that she might like my looks. I turned slowly and this time she didn't turn away, in fact she smiled, well, it was kind of like a "Mona Lisa" smile or it could have been gas, but anyway I smiled back at her. Suddenly I felt a spark inside of me. My pilot light had just been lit . . . forever!

After class we talked, her name was Teri. I asked her if I could call her and she declined, then I asked if I could walk her home and she declined once again. Finally I offered to walk her to her next class and she declined one last time. I turned and walked away . . . it must have been gas. A few weeks later a girl by the name of Nancy walked up to me. She was nice-looking, and smiling. The only reason I knew her name at all was because of roll call. She handed me a card, it was an invitation to a party on Friday night. "Vince, I sure would like you to come to my party, there'll be a lot of kids there, see you about seven," then she was gone. Walking quickly she handed a card to another boy that I didn't know. Being fresh from elementary school, the only parties I knew of were birthday parties, so I told Mom that I had to get this girl a birthday present. We hopped in the car and drove to the Osage Hills Shopping Center. Mom walked into C. R. Anthony's and returned with a wrapped gift in hand. Ha! I was all set for the party. Friday evening arrived, and freshly scrubbed and scented with Dad's Avon aftershave I walked the eight blocks to Nancy's house. She lived in a well-kept white frame house and I rang the doorbell. Nancy answered the door smiling as always, and I immediately handed her the gift. "Happy Birthday, Nancy!" I said beaming. For an instant she looked puzzled.

"Oh! It's not my birthday, Vince, it's just a party," she exclaimed.

"It's not?" I felt like a jerk, but I regrouped very well, "Well, keep the present anyway," I said, as if I were Diamond Jim. She graciously accepted the package and invited me in. I stepped inside and noticed some of my friends from school. They were drinking Cokes and eating cookies. Meanwhile all the girls in the room had followed Nancy out to the kitchen to watch her open her present. Suddenly we heard shrieks and screams coming from the kitchen and one little girl ran out into the dining room holding her mouth. What's wrong, I thought, and moved closer to the dining room. Suddenly I could hear the word, the reason for the shrieks and screams, the one word, the unbelievable word . . . PANTIES! OH MY GOD! Panties . . . where had I gone wrong? Why me? What had I ever done to anyone, other than my sister? What had my "soon to be deceased" mother done? I turned and walked to the nearest wall and rested my head on my forearm. I was ruined. I felt a light tap on my shoulder and turned to see Nancy standing before me.

"Thank you for the pa-pa-pa-panties," then she died laughing. Tears streamed from her eyes as she held her sides with both hands.

"You're wa-wa-wa-welcome" I said, and she pointed at me in silence. She couldn't catch her breath she was laughing so hard. But soon the laughter slowly died down and the record playing and dancing began. Later Nancy and I were slow-dancing and she thanked me again. "Oh, Vince, thank you for bringing that present. It was the hit of the party. I was afraid that my party would be a flop, but thanks to you it's great!"

So ends the tale of my first party, one I'll never forget.

The next morning our family left for a weekend in Okmulgee, Oklahoma. We arrived around ten o'clock and as we entered Grandma's camp house I could smell fresh bread baking. The smell of "sofky," which is hominy cooked together with hickory nut meats, hung in the air along with the aroma of coffee. Grandma's kitchen was a mixture of delicious scents, and secretly I wished that I could live with her and Grandpa. But I always felt out of place in the country. I had the same feeling when I was with Dad's family. I felt like an oddball, a boy without a race. I envied my Indian cousins and my Mexican cousins, for they were one race. They knew where they belonged. My Mexican cousins all spoke Spanish. My Indian cousins spoke no Creek but they lived the Indian life. And I lived the lifestyle of a white boy. I felt cursed, burdened. It was difficult for me, a teen, to fathom my life. I had been yanked out of a neighborhood where I was one of several Mexicans, and now I was in junior high with two other Mexican boys, Pete and Ray Gomez, and two Mexican girls, Linda and Olga Segovia, and a handful of Indian kids who seemed to disappear right after school was let out. I was never able to talk to them, they passed silently in the hallways. Only a nod of the head acknowledged my presence, and the knowledge that through our veins passed the blood of warriors . . . survivors. Even now as an adult the same holds true. Whether you are in a crowded mall, stuck in traffic, or at a feed store, anywhere predominantly white and black faces look at you, when one Indian spies another there is an immediate bonding that says "We are one."

I walked into the living room and saw Grandpa reading the Bible as he sat in his favorite chair. "Hi, Grandpa!" I said, but he never acknowledged me, he just kept reading. His response, or lack of it, did not surprise me. As far back as I could remember Grandpa McIntosh had never spoken more than three sentences to me. I walked on through the living room and out the front door. Butch and Brenda were not outside and then I remembered that they went to an all-Indian school in Tahlequah. I had wanted to go to school there too, but Mom wouldn't let me. I had met a Cherokee girl last summer and she had pleaded with me to join her.

The campgrounds were silent and I quickly grew bored. I looked out at the area where just last summer we had played ball. We boys had finally started growing muscles and the grounders and fly balls had a little sting to them as we caught them barehanded. I missed my cousins and I remembered the last time I had seen them. A rowdier bunch of kids you never saw, boy or girl, it didn't matter. Uncle Bill was the umpire, and our team was made up of cousins and the other team of kids from the other camp houses. Pug was pitching, William was playing first, I was on second, Butch was shortstop, and Brenda was playing third. The catcher and outfielders were little kids. Anyway, big Herschel Wolfe smashed a shot over the center fielder's head sending home the tying run from third. As he rounded second base digging for third, ornery Butch tackled him. Both benches cleared, the fight was on. Uncle Bill just laughed as kids wrestled on the ground, boys and girls fought as one. One older boy had Brenda down in a headlock and as he drew his hand back to smack her one, Vickie and little Marilyn grabbed his arm, and while Marilyn held his arm back, Vickie bit into his bicep and the big boy howled and two little Indian girls flew through the air as he jumped to his feet. By that time Brenda was on her feet and mad as all get out. She whipped the fire out of that boy with several slaps to the face and a swift kick to the groin. I chuckled as I thought of that last ball game and I walked out onto the dusty road that circled the campgrounds.

That night Grandpa's congregation had a singing. It was held outside around a big bonfire, and I listened from a distance to the magical songs sung in the Muskogee (Creek) language. The night was clear and a million stars shone as I sat alone in the dark listening to the wonderful-sounding language. The haunting melody rose to the heavens and in the distance I could hear a coyote howling as if it too wanted to join in the singing. Nowhere else in the entire world could I hear this sound. And I said aloud in the darkness, "How cool!" I thought of my Little Grandma and wondered what it would have been like one hundred years before, trying to outrun Confederate soldiers.

Once again I wished that I had been born in those days of adventure and excitement. As I listened to the language of my ancestors being sung I felt a distinct awareness come over me and fill me with pride. I was Indian! I looked to the heavens and said softly, "Thank you, Little Grandma."

Back in Tulsa, Monday morning came early and as Arnold and I walked up to a group of our friends they handed us each a flyer. We read the flyer anxiously. It was about playing football. Hot dog! This was more like it. All day long we boys could talk of nothing but football. Within the week we were all suited up, knowing that some day we would be "Hall of Famers," not to be confused with a "Hall of Farmers," which would be more likely. Wearing our pads proudly, like the armor of knights of old, we walked out onto the practice field ready for mortal combat. Bring on Notre Dame, the Packers. Ha! Bring on the Colts! We the mighty "Roosevelt Rough Riders" spit on your ugly black hightop shoes! "Wait, what was that, coach . . . five laps? What? You mean we gotta run?" Henry Topchak stood with his whistle in his mouth. He wore a gray sweatshirt, blue jeans, and sneakers. He watched as his seventh-grade team staggered by him. Only four more laps to go. By the fourth lap Henry Topchak's season was already over; for some reason he was reminded of the Bataan Death March as his winded Rough Riders flopped in the grass like a group of beached whales. But youth being what it is, in a matter of days we were up to snuff. Throwing each other in the dirt, dog-piling, spitting, learning new swear words by the day . . . it was great!

Our pads were okay, but everyone had on different colored pants, and the helmets . . . woof! They were plastic, no chin straps, no face mask, no nothing. We looked like the Little Rascals! Coach Top, as we called him, had me playing right guard on offense and defense. But this practice he wanted to try me in the backfield, so he moved me to fullback. I was all set to run against two of the biggest twelve-year-olds in the city. "Baby Huey" was what we called one of them, and he loved it. He stood six feet, one inch and weighed two hundred twelve pounds. The other kid was "Whammy." His real name was Sammy, but at six feet, one inch and two hundred fifteen pounds, "Whammy" was more appropriate. I took the handoff and ran toward the towering monsters. I sidestepped Whammy, but Baby Huey nailed me high on the chest and drove me into the ground. Coach Top yelled at me, "No, no, no! Bend over and duck your head, then drive with your legs! Here give me the ball, I'll show you.'' I tossed him the ball and he walked to where I had stood. The two monsters returned to their position. "Now when I run at you, you two men try to stop me," Coach Top shouted. The monsters looked at each other, then smiled. Hut one, hut two, Coach Top was off like a shot. Whammy hit him low and Baby Huey hit him high driving him back over Whammy . . . CRAAAAAACK! All else was silent as Coach Top let out the most blood curdling scream I had ever heard! I looked at him as he lay crying in pain, a bone protruded through his blue jeans just below his left knee! Coach Bill dashed to his side; he yelled for one of the boys to run across the street to the Owen Park Recreation Center and call an ambulance.

A week later I was invited to another party, and I knew that it wasn't a birthday party. Ha! I was getting the hang of this party life, but of course even if it had been a birthday party I wouldn't have brought a present. Arnold's mom dropped us off at Mary Shelton's house and the football players mingled with the other boys and girls. The living room was dark and cozy, music was playing, and in the dining room chips and dip adorned the table. Arnold and I were talking with Welby London, our team center, about football. Suddenly I felt a tap on my shoulder. It was Mary, the hostess. "Vince, can I talk to you?"

"Sure," I said, as I stepped away from my friends.

"See that girl over there," she pointed to an attractive brunette who stood with two other young girls. The attractive girl looked at me and smiled. I smiled back and the girl continued to stare at me.

"What about her?"

"Her name is Chrissy Linns and she likes you."

"Likes me. I don't even know her."

"She wants to dance with you."

"Okay, yeah, maybe later."

Mary grabbed me by my arm, like any good future fixer-upper. "Vee-yunce," she pleaded with her eyes, "she likes you," then she raised her eyebrows up and down.

"Ohhhh, she likes me," I said, and Mary released my arm and laughed, "Yes, now go dance." Then she quickly walked away to match someone else.

I walked back over to Arnold and Welby. As I listened to football and baseball statistics from them, I glanced over at the girl named Chrissy. She was sitting down now, but she continued to smile at me. Oh heck, I might as well get this over with and maybe she'll leave me alone. Little did I know that this would be my last rational act for the next three years. I walked across the room to where she sat. As I got closer to her I couldn't believe my eyes, she was beautiful, absolutely gorgeous! Holy Moly! I introduced myself and as luck would have it someone played a slow dance. I looked over at the record player and there stood "Little Miss Matchmaker" Mary grinning like a Cheshire cat. I shook my head and she waved at me, then she was off to ruin someone else's life. I slipped my arm around Chrissy's waist, then caught the seductive fragrance of her perfume. Wow! Something strange happened, I didn't know what it was, but it felt like my pilot light kicked on a burner. We were dancing cheek to cheek; my heart quickened as I felt her smooth skin next to mine. I drew back from her and looked into her hazel eyes, then I looked at her red lips. She smiled, revealing perfect white teeth, and the second burner came on, something was happening in my shorts, but I didn't know what! I didn't care!

"A penny for your thoughts," she said softly.

THOUGHTS! THOUGHTS! I didn't even know my own name at this point! I looked at her and said, "Haruna gonna wah," which caught us both by surprise. "What?" she said, as she searched my face for a translation. I cleared my throat, "Nice party, huh?" There, that was better.

"Oh, yes, yes it is now," she said as she pulled me closer to her. She looked into my eyes and moved her lips close to mine, then she tilted her head ever so slightly, and closed her eyes. Holy Moly! She wants me to kiss her! Kiss her! Now? I had only kissed old what's-her-name and what's-her-face and you-know-who . . . God I couldn't even remember their names. I tilted my head and slowly moved my lips toward hers. I closed my eyes as our lips met. This was better than baseball or football, it was even better than hamburgers! For the next three years my hormone levels flourished. It was great!

One of my classes at Roosevelt Junior High was band. I enjoyed band and I especially liked the instructor, Frank Chilton. He was of average height and sported a flattop hair-cut. We called him Frankenstein, because of his name and his hair-cut. We drove him bonkers, and yet this man had more impact on me than he would ever know. We were a rowdy group of teens, and someone in our class would get a swat daily. But Frankenstein endured. He taught us etiquette, dress, responsibility, courage, and oh yes, music. I saw him save the life of one of my classmates one day. She had a seizure in the hallway, and from out of nowhere came Mr. Chilton. Like Superman himself, he worked with the girl while I ran for help. When I returned to the hallway, I saw him scoop her up in his arms and carry her to the nurse's office. He was quite a man in my book, and I hoped that I would be much like him when I grew older. I wanted to tell him that I really admired him, but I could never find the courage. I mean we were a rowdy class and I guess I let peer pressure keep me from it. He moved away during my ninth-grade year. And now as an adult, when I hear a school band play I think of Mr. Chilton, and I kick myself for not telling him "thank you."

My musical experience was just getting off the ground as "El 16 de Septiembre" passed. This was the major celebration of the year for the Mexican community in Tulsa. It commemorated Mexico's independence from Spain in 1821. The Mendoza family played for the fiesta, as they had for the past thirty years. Also celebrated was "Cinco de Mayo," which commemorated Mexico's stubborn defense of Puebla from the invading French in 1862. My two favorite people at the fiesta were Salud and Tony Silva. Dad and Tony had played baseball together as children, and later worked in the coal mines together in order to survive. Dad had the highest respect for Tony, and when he told me stories of their youth he would always end it by saying, "Tony Silva is the finest man I've ever known." Tony was short, dark, and very soft-spoken. Salud was short too but fair-skinned and quite the talker, and I loved to hear her talk. Every time I saw her she would ask the same question in her loud voice, "How you was Vicente? And how's you Mama and Daddy?" She and Tony were the two sweetest people on earth, and they loved each other dearly. At the fiesta Tony would recite a patriotic verse and Salud would give a patriotic speech, ending it with "Viva Mexico!" The audience would respond by yelling, "Viva!" She would do this three times, then take her bow and leave the stage. I'll never forget Salud and Tony Silva.

The band played a lot of dances at the local VFW on Sixth Street. Uncle Claude would rent the hall from the veterans and then spread the word, and the Mexican community would arrive on Saturday night ready to dance. It was a happy time, never any trouble because most of the Mexican people had come to Oklahoma together, working the fields or coal mines during the Great Depression. They were all friends, they had all known hard times. My favorite male singer was my Uncle Claude, but we were soon joined by another Mendoza. His name was Victor. He wasn't related to us, but he was quite the singer and guitarist. He had won Arthur Godfrey's talent show on national television, and he was a real celebrity in Tulsa. I liked Victor a lot, but I would grow to hate his name. Since Victor and Vincent both start with the letter V, and since he was the most celebrated Mendoza in Tulsa County, I would be called Victor by every Anglo-type person I met for the next two thousand years. Secretly I wished his parents had named him Bubba. My favorite female singers were my Cousin Veda and my Tía (Aunt) Connie. They only knew one song together and that was "Dame Cuenta de Tu Vida" (Give me an account of your life). They really sounded good. Veda was bashful and when the song was over she would turn a deep red and walk off the stage waving and smiling. Aunt Connie sang very well and I never could understand why she didn't sing more songs with her brothers. I had to admit that she and Uncle Joe really looked cool when they danced together, they were smooth as silk, and I would always look for them on the crowded dance floor. Dad on the other hand was not a dancer. He thought he was, and on certain occasions he would leave the bandstand and rush to Mom and they would dance together . . . how embarrassing! He danced like Groucho Marx walked! Crouched down and head up just like a turkey. Oh my God! Mom's face would be red as Dad crouched this way and that way, turning and spinning. All he needed was a cigar hanging out of his mouth. Everyone smiled at them, and shook their heads. Concho Mendoza was cutting a rug! I heard Linda ask Mama one time after a dance, "Mama, why did you marry him?" and Mama just laughed.

We played music at several private parties also. My favorite was at the home of businessman Walter Helmerich. He was a wealthy man, and he was a nice person. Everyone in the band liked him because he spoke Spanish, and he knew what he sang. He called Uncle Claude "Pancho," and Uncle Claude would laugh heartily. When Mr. Helmerich walked away Uncle Claude would call him a name in Spanish, and everyone in the band would laugh. Mr. Helmerich knew the words to some Mexican songs, and he pronounced them perfectly, that was what endeared him to the band. He sang with gusto and feeling; he sang from the heart was what Uncle Claude said about him, and everyone in the band agreed.

Christmas was fast approaching, and a pretty Christmas tree stood in the corner next to our fake fireplace. The Christmas lights blinked off and on, bubbles made their way to the tops of liquid-filled lights, silver icicles hung on every branch as the smell of fresh tamales filled the house. Every Christmas the Mexican families of Tulsa would fix tamales, this was a tradition that was well worth waiting for. Oh, the smell of masa and pork, along with each individual's secret ingredients to make them as original as an artist's name on his work! Served with the tamales would be beans and the Spanish rice Waleeta (Grandma Mendoza) called "sopa." No one has ever fixed rice the way Waleeta did.

Mama too always made tamales at Christmas time. My Waleeta had taught Mama how to cook Mexican food and Mama had caught on fast. She could hold her own with any first-generation Mexican that sauntered into Oklahoma. Waleeta showed her the ingredients and how much to use, and just like her Mama never wrote anything down, she kept it all in her head. And every Christmas Mama, Waleeta, Aunt Connie, and Aunt Julia would have a secret contest to see who made the best tamales in the family. Nothing was announced, it was all done by eye contact. Hell hath no fury like a woman's tamale scorned! I felt truly sorry for Uncle Joe, Uncle Claude, and Dad. Uncle Joe would bite into one of Mama's tamales and say, "Mmm, these are good, Martha." Mama would smile as Aunt Connie's eyes clicked toward Uncle Joe, and Uncle Joe, slick diplomat that he was, would counter with "But I believe that Connie's got you beat on this particular batch." Then he'd turn his head and wink at me, as Connie smiled and told everyone that this wasn't her really best batch. Meanwhile, Mama would be smiling at Aunt Connie and acting like it was no big deal. Dad would pick up his plate and leave the room. Uncle Pancho was the true politico: "They all taste the same to me!" he'd insist, and the competitors would glare at him and mumble to themselves.

Christmas Eve was always spent at home with the family. Christmas Day we would all drive to Okmulgee to have Christmas with Grandma and Grandpa McIntosh. The family was so large that everyone chose to draw names for Christmas gifts. We kids had fun just being with each other again.

In Tulsa I knelt beside the Christmas tree and browsed through the brightly wrapped gifts searching for the ones with my name on them. I would shake each one and try to guess what was inside. Like every kid in America, I thought Christmas was my favorite time of the year.

I missed the old neighborhood and occasionally Dad would take me back to see my Waleeta. She would cry, "Mi hijo" (My son), and I would hug her as she wrapped both arms around my waist. I was just thirteen, but already I was a head taller than her. She'd blow her nose into her white hanky, then she'd take my hand and lead me into the kitchen. She'd pull out a chair for me, walk back to the stove, and go on making tortillas. She'd turn and look at me, shake her head and smile, and say something to Daddy, and Dad would tell me what she said. Usually it was, "He's so big," or "He's growing too fast." When we left, she would stand on her porch and wave her white hanky at us until we were out of sight. Waleeta died two years later. I remember coming home from school, Mom and Dad were in the kitchen when they told me that my Waleeta had died in the hospital. The news surprised me and I walked out the back door and went to Dad's workshop. I closed the door behind me and stood there thinking about my grandma. I cried softly so that no one would hear me, no one except my Waleeta.

It was the spring of 1961 and boys were beginning to call on my sister . . . good Grief! My sister was by no means a "Sandra Dee," not a flashy sort of person, but Lordy, the guys that showed up on our doorstep! For a while I thought some practical joker had painted "Mission" on our front door. I saw all kinds of guys. I had never seen a Mexican geek before, but once when I answered the door, there he stood in all his glory. Most Mexican guys are pretty macho, especially the short ones. This guy was something else. He had on a white shirt, with brown slacks pulled up five inches above his navel. He wore brown shoes and white socks . . . oy!

"Iss Leenda home?" he asked.

"Jes," I said, mimicking Bill Dana, who did José Jimenez on the radio. "Come on in."

He smiled and stepped into our living room. I turned and yelled to my sis, "Oh, Leeeeeenda!" I heard her scream in the back room, then I heard the thud, thud, thud of her dainty feet and I ran out to the front porch. I heard someone else in the living room with Carlos. The voice was sweet and bubbly, so happy and carefree. I tiptoed back to the front door and peeked into the living room to see who it could be . . . it was Leeenda. I couldn't believe that this was the very same person who had tied me to Mama's bedpost and crammed watermelon down my throat just because I cried for the last piece. And now she was trying to act like Shelly Fabares on *The Donna Reed Show.* Ha! Girls, they were sly. I saw that they were getting ready to leave and I ran off the porch and onto the lawn. As Carlos and Leenda came down the front steps, she turned her head toward me and and mouthed the word "Stupid."

"Adios, Leeenda!" I said, and I heard her say to Carlos in her sweet, sweet voice, "Isn't he silly." Carlos opened the car door for her and when he shut it and walked around the car, Leenda looked at me with puckered mouth and squinted eyes. I died laughing. Carlos started the engine on his Rambler, and it jumped, smoked, and lurched down the block and around the corner. I was rolling on the ground as Leenda held on for dear life.

The next guy was Dan Ochoa. I liked Dan. He drove a hot red '57 Chevy coupe. It was skirted and had chrome everywhere, and a set of pipes that rumbled low and mean. It was bad. He also had a nice-looking sister named Laura, but she was too old for me, or so she said. I did manage to make some change off my sister. Mom and Dad made me go on dates with Linda if they were to drive-in movies, and I was a pro at pestering both Linda and her date to no end. I'd make sure that I never stopped talking, then casually mention to the unsuspecting victim that I'd probably enjoy myself much better if I sat in the lawn chairs that were placed outside and in front of the snack bar. The guy would tell me to go ahead if I wanted to, thinking that he had slicked me into leaving. I'd start to open the door, and the guy always had a gleam in his eyes when I did that. I'd stop as I touched the door handle. "I think I'll need about five dollars for popcorn, candy and a drink," I would say, smiling at him. The victim would smile back through clenched teeth, and dig frantically for his wallet while I held my enterprising young hand out for my five simoleons. I was quite the polite little extortionist as I thanked him for his business. I did very well that spring.

Linda was getting ready to graduate from Central High School. It was a true miracle in my estimation, but she was the scholar of our family . . . she studied. I on the other hand listened in school, but when three o'clock came, school was over. Finito, sayonara, adios muchacho! I sat in the dining room watching as Mom helped Linda with her graduation cap and gown. Dad fumbled and grumbled with the cheapola camera that he had bought at a pawn shop. I knew what was going to happen. I shook my head and continued to watch as Linda sat in a chair to pose for a picture.

Dad looked at her and began yelling, "No, no, no. Don't sit like that, sit like this!" He hurried over and showed her how he wanted her to sit. Linda started sniffling. I knew it was all over. She wasn't tough like me. I had toughened up after years of being yelled at. The old-timer's words rolled off me like water off a duck's back, but Linda couldn't take it. For the first time in my life I felt sorry for my sister. Dad stomped back to his original position, then yelled, "Smile." All I could hear was Linda crying, and Mom rushed to her and tried to console her. Meanwhile, Dad was stomping around in a circle in the living room. An hour later the photo session was over, and Linda ran to her room and threw herself on the bed. "I hate him, I hate him!" she cried into her pillow and I slowly walked over and sat by her on the edge of the bed. I patted her back, "Don't worry, Sis, when you graduate you can get out of here," I paused for a moment, "Great, then I'll be stuck with him." She laughed through her tears and then sat up and wiped her eyes and looked at me. Suddenly she hugged me and patted my back, and for the first time in my life I hugged my sister.

Linda started dating an older fellow, his name was Ronnie Dellinger, who worked at the same place that Linda did. He was nice enough, in fact lately he was the only one that looked and acted halfway normal. The only thing I didn't like about him was his size. He was a little guy. My heroes were John Wayne and Johnny Unitas. Linda had dated a couple of big guys, but they didn't have much on the ball, so much for brawn. Ronnie and I got along okay, in fact he taught me how to drive his Ford Falcon station wagon. It was a standard shift and I did pretty well around the neighborhood. One day after he and Linda announced their engagement we were out driving and I pulled over to the curb and shut off the engine. Ronnie looked at me strangely as I turned my head to look at him. "Do you really love her, Ronnie?"

"Yes, Vince, I do."

"That's good," I said, and I paused for a moment. "She's kind of stupid about some things. There's one thing I've got to let you know."

"What's that, Vince?"

"She's my sister. If you ever lay a hand on her you'll have me to answer to." I looked him straight in the eye.

"Oh, Vince, you don't need to worry about that. My dad didn't raise us boys to be mean."

"Well I just want you to know where I stand."

Ronnie looked at his watch. "We better get going, I bet Martha's got supper ready for us." I quickly started the engine and we hurried home to one of Mama's fantastic meals.

On 21 November 1961 Ronnie and Linda were married at the Osage

Hills Christian Church. As I watched her come down the aisle I got a lump in my throat. She actually looked kind of pretty. I remembered her waking me in the middle of the night when we lived on North Quincy and I had to get dressed to go to the bathroom with her; she was afraid to walk to the outhouse in the dark. I would stand outside in the rain or sleet while she did her business, then together we would slog back through the muck and mire to our couch that folded out to a bed. I thought about the story Mom told of her when she was going to Longfellow Elementary School. Some kids had been making fun of Junior and she beat them with her lunch pail. When she came home that day her lunch pail was all bent and dented. The kids never picked on Junior after that. I remembered our last encounter just a few weeks before. I had found Linda washing dishes in the kitchen and noticed a large cake cover and a big metal spoon on our dining table. Ha! I tiptoed up behind Linda, cake cover in my left hand, the huge spoon in the other. As she reached her hands into the water, quick as a flash I placed the cake cover over her head and banged it four times with the large spoon. I took off like a shot for the back door and just as I jerked it open a five-pound skillet sailed by my head and bounced off the wall! I dashed from the back porch laughing wildly.

Now as they repeated their vows before their friends I grew sad. Linda was off on a new adventure. She was gone forever and I felt like I was losing my best friend. Then suddenly I perked up . . . hey! I get her room! The sadness vanished and a wicked smile crossed my face. As they completed their vows, in my mind I was already redecorating my new bedroom.

FOUR // Me and the Guys

We played a lot of baseball that summer. Of course we did that every summer, and our team was quite good. We usually won the city championship every year while I was growing up. I got over being nervous when Dad showed up for a game, which wasn't very often. But my true love was football. When school started in September I found that I had developed speed . . . blinding speed. I didn't realize it then, but my neighborhood was a perfect training site. Steep hills and rolling hills, and of course I ran or rode my bicycle everywhere I went. I was building strength and endurance without even realizing it.

As we ran wind sprints I easily bested my classmates, much to the pleasure of Coach Topchak. Later he praised me for my speed and ability to catch a football. As we practiced I could hear him telling the other coaches about my ability, and I felt good inside. According to Top we would take the city championship with ease this year. One week before the season was to start Coach Top called me over to him. "Vince, I'm sorry, but you're going to have to move up to the varsity team because of your age."

"Come on, Coach, these are my friends. I don't want to play with those other guys."

"Sorry, Vince. I don't want to give you up either, but rules are rules. Go over and check in with Coach Burns, he'll be glad to see you."

I slowly walked over to my new coach. He didn't act too impressed with me. I practiced hard and held my own with the guys, but he only played me two or three downs a game. Meanwhile the junior varsity was going undefeated. In fact we scrimmaged the junior varsity and they beat us. My eighth-grade year was quite a disappointment as far as football was concerned.

On the other hand there were benefits to being a football player. Cheerleaders! I went through them like a hot knife through butter. So sweet, so delicate, so sexy! I was a year older than my pals and I guess that ac-

counted for my head being in the clouds for those junior high days. Hor-
mones racing, I loved my way through the eighth grade.

August 1962 arrived. I donned my shoulder pads and helmet and
dreamed of playing for the University of Oklahoma. In my backyard
stood half a dozen pop bottles spaced three feet apart. I would run at full
speed, cutting this way and that, practicing my footwork. I had watched
the likes of Prentice Gault and Tommy McDonald, who played for the
University of Oklahoma, but my true idol was Willie Gallimore, who
played for the Chicago Bears. I loved to watch him run, and I wanted to
run just like him. I ran everywhere I went, and as an eighth grader I'd
been dubbed the fastest kid in school. Our ninth-grade coach was a man
named Eskell Frazier. He was a good man. He was straightforward, and if
you weren't doing your job he'd sure let you know about it. I can still see
him standing there on the field. He wore work shoes, khaki pants, check-
ered shirt, and a red baseball cap. We'd do anything for the man.

I also returned punts and kickoffs, or at least I tried. The other teams
would never kick to my side of the field, and later I found out that they
were sending men out to scout us. About that time another Creek boy on
the other side of town was making a name for himself in football. His
name was Joey Grayson. I had played baseball and basketball against
him, he didn't impress me any. We played a black team called the Carver
Cats. We had the ball on their forty-two-yard line and our quarterback
called my number. It was a pitch out to the right side. I ran a touchdown
on that play, and it was called back because our center, Welby London,
was fighting with their linebacker. I told Bobby to give me the ball again
on the same play. He did and I ran it in again for another touchdown. At
halftime Welby complained to Coach Frazier, "Hey, Coach, those guys
have mustaches and beards," and we all laughed. On one play during the
second half their halfback flew out of their backfield and down the sidelines. I took a quick glance over my left shoulder to see if I had any help
coming, but no one was in sight. I was the only man between the big runner and the goal line. I ran at him at full speed, closing the distance fast. I
zeroed in on his belt in case he tried to head-fake me. As we closed the
distance to three yards we each ducked our head, he intent on running
over me, and I intent on driving him into the ground. Our heads clashed
together like two mountain rams and our bodies fell limp into the grass.
We had knocked each other out. After the game I noticed that part of the
webbing inside my helmet had been broken. The next practice I donned a

new helmet and by week's end it had cracked in two. I was ducking my head when tackled, not realizing what damage I was doing to the bones in my neck.

On 24 November 1962 Diana Lynn Dellinger was born. I was an uncle! Mom and Dad were on cloud nine as we stared at the bundle of joy with the full head of black hair. Ronnie and Linda lived on what native Tulsans called the Sand Springs line, actually Charles Page Boulevard, which was just a few blocks from our house. If Mom or Dad weren't bowling they could be found changing diapers and playing with the baby. She was a darling little girl and when she began to walk she and I went everywhere. It felt good to have Dina, as I called her, run to me with open arms whenever she saw me. She was a sweetheart.

One day after practice I noticed four Indian boys standing near the sidelines. I walked over to them thinking how strange it was to see them at the football field. I knew one of them, and he spoke to me.

"Hi, Vince, how ya doing?"

"Fine, fine, what's up, Cordell?"

"Well, me and the guys," and he motioned to his friends, "we'd like to know if you'd run in a track meet for Bowen Indian Baptist Church?"

"When is it?"

"This Saturday."

I thought a moment, and with nothing else planned I agreed to run for the church. The Indian boys shook my hand and smiled. I would meet them at Webster Stadium at eight o'clock Saturday morning. Saturday arrived, and as I stepped from Dad's car an Indian man walked toward me. He favored my father a lot. His name was Eugene Alford, he was the coach for the Indian team. The track meet was open to any Christian athlete in Tulsa who had yet to graduate from high school. I was nervous as I looked at the bigger stronger boys, but I was willing to do my part for the Indian church. I entered the hundred-yard dash and placed second. Not bad for a flatlander in tennis shoes. Next I placed third in the shotput, second in the broad jump, second in the two-hundred-twenty-yard dash, and then we entered the four-man quarter-mile relay. Coach Alford wanted me to run the first leg, but I wanted to run the anchor. He talked me into running the first leg because he wanted to get a big jump on the field. I agreed and took my place in the starting blocks. As I kicked each leg trying to relax the muscles I heard someone yelling from the front row, a few feet away. It was an old white man. He was little and wiry, with a stubble of gray whiskers on his face.

"C'mon Injun, you can do it! Show them dang white boys what ya got! You can do it boy!"

I grinned at him as his embarrassed daughter tried to quiet him, and the crowd chuckled. He waved his worn hat at me. "Go get 'em, boy!" he yelled as the starter called us to the blocks. When the gun sounded I heaved my body up and took several short steps to get going, but as I took my first power stride I saw my foot go across the white stripe. I had committed a foul. I stopped dead in my tracks and the other boys passed me. I turned around and glanced at the starter, who shook his head as he looked at me. I knew that I had disqualified the team. I turned and sprinted to catch the pack. I took the lead just as it was time to pass the baton to the next runner and a roar went up from the crowd. I passed the baton clean to Billy Elk, who got us a ten-yard lead, then he passed it to Les Sampson, who lost five yards. Tommie White Crow waited with his arm outstretched as Les came huffing and puffing into the final relay. It was a clean handoff, Tommy turned it on and one hundred ten yards later he had won by twenty yards. The stadium roared and the little white man who had yelled at me was dancing a jig on the track. Then came the announcement. We had been disqualified by my stepping across the line. I felt terrible, but there was nothing that I could do. I ran to the starter and pleaded my case, "Hey, I gave them a thirty-yard head start. Give us a break, huh?"

"Sorry, son, rules are rules."

The next event was the mile run. Only two boys entered and the guys wanted me to enter because I could do no worse than third place and I was sure to get another ribbon at the awards ceremony. But I declined, I felt too rotten. I had let my friends down and it gnawed at me. The awards ceremony was to be held on a Thursday night. I had a football game, so Millie Stiles, a friend of mine from Roosevelt, said she would be happy to accept the awards for me. The next morning she handed me my ribbons and proudly announced to me that all the judges agreed that I would be the next Jim Thorpe. That was quite a compliment. I smiled as I looked at the ribbons. Maybe I'd make it to the University of Oklahoma after all.

We were doing our pregame exercises for the big game against Hamilton Junior High. Our offensive line averaged two hundred thirty pounds, and theirs was roughly the same. I glanced over at Steve Mulligan, a third-string halfback. He looked worried.

"Hey Steve, be cool man, you can't get hurt playing this game."

"Sure, Vince, sure," was all he said as Coach Frazier called us to a team huddle. "All right, you guys, we need this game! I want one hundred and ten percent out of each and every one of you! Now let's go get 'em!" We broke the huddle and ran out on the field seeking glory, as parents and friends cheered from the stands. The night was crisp and the smell of popcorn and hot coffee filled the air.

We played hard, harder than we had ever played before, but late in the fourth quarter the game was still scoreless. Coach Frazier pulled me out of the game for a few downs. He chewed me out for not hustling on the end sweeps. I told him I'd do better and he sent me back in. A few plays later we turned the ball over to the other team. As I readied myself for defense I heard someone call my name. I turned and saw Steve Mulligan running toward me. Boy, I must have really screwed up if Mulligan was taking my place.

"Coach wants you out," he said, and I immediately trotted toward our sideline. Five yards from the line everything turned upside down in my vision and I dropped to the ground. I remember hearing a woman scream, then suddenly I found myself looking up into the faces of Coach Frazier and my teammates. An ambulance was called and later I found myself lying in a hospital room. Chrissy rode with me in the ambulance, and shortly after I changed into my hospital gown she was allowed to enter my room.

She came in cautiously. "Are you feeling better?"

"Yeah, I feel okay."

"You look so cute in that white gown. You look just like a little monkey," she said smiling lovingly.

"Thanks, thanks a lot," I said as she leaned over and gave me a kiss. She looked cute in her cheerleader outfit and I was glad she was my girl. She was a sweetheart. I was really crazy about her. Coach Frazier and my parents arrived at the same time. After a brief exam by an emergency doctor my parents were told that they would have to leave and I spent the night alone, never realizing that my future as a football player was over. I was told that I'd had a mild concussion. A few days later I returned to school. I was talking with my friends between classes when the world suddenly turned upside down and I fell hard to the wooden floor. I awoke in the hospital. A group of neurosurgeons checked me for over a week. They found nothing but a concussion and sent me home. It was while I was at home that the headaches began. Not mild headaches but massive pain, almost unbearable. Pain pills did nothing and Dad was putting ice pack after ice pack on my head to no avail. Finally one day in an attempt to stop my anguish he placed the ice pack under my neck, right at the base of my skull. The relief was almost instant. I sighed and breathed deeply as the pain subsided. I had been without sleep for three days and as I felt the darkness approaching I relaxed and let it envelop me. Dad took me to his chiropractor, a kindly old gentleman. As soon as I removed the ice pack from my neck the throbbing pain slowly started. The old doctor felt my neck, talking to himself as he examined me. "Uh huh, mmm, my goodness, mmm, okay. Young man your vertebrae are all jammed up. I'm going to get rid of that headache for you right now. Lie down on this table." He pulled gently on my neck, twisted it this way and that, tugged gently, and then suddenly tugged and jerked my head at the same time. I felt a tremendous crack and a sharp pain, then relief. He felt my neck again.

"There, that's the way they are supposed to be. How do you feel?"

"I feel great, the headache is gone!"

I returned home, but I was still depressed. The doctor had said no more football for that year, and Mom had begged me to quit while I was moaning in pain during my ordeal, and I had agreed; now I had to honor my word. The thing I loved most in the whole world had been taken from me. I loved the roughness of the sport. The running, the hitting, the sweating, and the blood. It was like an intoxicating elixir. The elixir of raw power. Strength, speed, and agility, I had it all, but now it was all gone. The hardest thing to do was check in my gear. It seemed like a part of myself had been severed. As I watched my friends practice I felt nauseated. Why me, God? I wanted to be the first Mexican Indian to play football at the University of Oklahoma. I wanted the Mexican and Indian children to know that they could be stars. Jim Thorpe was not the only great Indian athlete in the world. There were others, but that list wouldn't include me. I tried running a few weeks later. My speed was gone. I was average again. Meanwhile, across town Joey Grayson was setting the stage to become one of Tulsa's premier running backs. A month after I quit the football team, Chrissy left me for a guitar player. It had all been a game to her, and this only added to my woes.

I continued to play basketball and baseball, but my coordination had left me. I was never any good at basketball in the first place, and it was hard to believe that I could actually get worse, but I did. Baseball was the same story. Spring arrived and I looked forward to tossing the ball around with the guys. I knew something was wrong when I couldn't judge a fly ball. My God, I had been playing since the third grade and now I couldn't judge a pop-up. I envied Arnold, he was a good steady little ball player at any sport. I was really down. I had never sat the bench during a baseball game and now I found myself "riding the pine" and I didn't like it. I could hit the ball all right, and I considered myself a dang good hitter, but my fielding had left me along with my legs.

It was April 1963 and Don Howard, a classmate, invited a bunch of us guys out to his grandfather's farm near Skiatook, Oklahoma. Since most of us had been Boy Scouts together we eagerly accepted his invitation. We packed our gear into two station wagons and Don's parents took eight of us out to the farm and dropped us off. We had three pup tents, and rations and water for two days. We waved goodbye to Don's parents and then with gear in hand we started into the woods to find a good camp area. All my friends were white boys. We had been together since Pershing Elementary and I thought of them as almost brothers. We had shared our entire childhood. We found a good area by a muddy creek and began pitching camp. We all helped with camp chores. Two boys dug a latrine, two collected firewood and dug a small pit for the fires, and four of us set up the three pup tents. After everything was done we flipped coins to see who got to sleep in the tents. Arnold and I shared one, Butch Tilton and Don Howard shared the second, and the last tent went to Welby London and Steve Mulligan. Perry Sparks and Bill Decker would have to sleep by the fire. They were both hat nuts; Bill was wearing a floppy roll-up sort of golf hat, and Perry sported a black derby that his uncle had brought him from England. Bill was short and had thin short brown hair, while Perry was tall, with a face full of freckles and brown hair. They hated each other, but I liked both of them. Don Howard was short, with brown hair. He played right halfback, and safety with me on the football team. Butch Tilton was real small, blond, blue-eyed, and he sported a flattop haircut. He played drums in the school band. Welby London was tall and husky, the biggest and the nicest guy of the whole gang. Steve Mulligan was real quiet. He was of average height, with just a sprinkling of freckles on his nose. He wanted to be tough, but he just didn't have the look in his eyes. Once we were settled in we went fishing, and after an hour of no bites we set off on a hike. Off into the boonies we marched. That too turned out to be uneventful so we returned to camp and had lunch. It was kind of boring until the sun set, and then things went bonkers. As the sun dropped beneath the horizon we lit the two Coleman lanterns that we had brought along. Arnold and I added wood to one fire and Welby and Steve did the same for the other. Just then a screech owl cut loose and sixteen eyeballs searched the darkness. Coyotes howled in the distance and Steve swore they were timber wolves. He pulled his BB gun from his bedroll, and Arnold and I looked at each other and shook our heads. Right, like a BB gun is going to stop a wolf, or even a bunny rabbit.

Butch crawled into his tent and pulled out several packs of cigars. He passed them out like he was a brand new dad, and we each thanked him and lit up. The cigar added to the experience. Here we were out in the Wild West sitting by the camp fire smoking stogies. The night air was crisp and Bill filled his metal cup with water and set it in the coals of the fire to heat for hot chocolate. Seeing this we began to prepare our supper. Arnold and I had brought a couple of steaks, we were the envy of the camp. Butch had peanut butter and jelly sandwiches, and the others had cold cuts. Right after supper we heard the coyotes and they were close, real close. Then Don spoke up, "Hey Steve let's go pop those coyotes with your gun." Steve's mouth dropped open. Then I spoke.

"I'll go with you guys if you want to go."

"That's great, let's go," Don replied, and Steve slowly stood up with a sick look on his face. Ten minutes later we were walking down a narrow road. There was barbwire fencing on each side. The moon was full and we could see fairly well. We heard a low distant rumbling. We stopped and listened. The rumbling grew louder. Suddenly, fifty yards away we saw a herd of horses bearing down on us, there must have been fifty of them running at a full gallop. Don took off first and I turned to run too, but something made me look over my shoulder and to my horror I saw Steve Mulligan trip and fall. I was five yards from him, and the horses were now thirty yards away. Damn, this was like some movie. I cursed under my breath and ran to Steve. He stood up, but he had sprained his ankle. The horses were right on top of us when I grabbed him by his belt with one hand and his shirt collar with the other. I picked him up and threw him over the top strand of wire and held on, all in one motion, and as we hit the ground the fifty horses ran by us while we lay in the dirt huffing and puffing. "Jesus," he said. Just then Don yelled at us.

"Hey! Are you guys all right?"

We didn't answer, we were still a little dazed.

"Man, that was cool, Vince," Don said, as I slowly got to my feet. I reached my hand out and Steve grabbed it and I pulled him up. "I think we better get back to camp," I said and Steve draped one arm over my shoulder and one over Don's shoulder. We were almost back to camp when we stopped in our tracks. There was a light moving across the pasture. It was moving fast, we wondered what it could be. Five seconds later we heard an awful scream, it sounded like a mountain lion, it continued to scream, then we heard the mountain lion cussing. I took off for the light as Don helped Steve back to camp. I couldn't believe my eyes when I got to the light. It was Butch Tilton carrying a Coleman lantern and he was naked as a picked bird! He was also cut and bleeding. He had run into a barbwire fence at full speed! Just then Welby and Perry arrived. We picked Butch up and carried him back to camp. When we arrived Bill had cut down a small tree so that it would fall across the fire, and the camp was lit up. We bandaged Butch with Band-Aids and strips of our T-shirts. He looked like a deranged mummy, but he was okay. We asked what he was doing naked out in the field. He and Perry had been playing strip poker and the loser had to run across the field to a pine tree and bring back a pine cone to prove that he had made the trip. Unfortunately for Butch there was a fence on the way. Butch sat on a log by the fire. Suddenly he cried out and hobbled toward the fallen tree, reached down, and pulled his melted fishing pole from the fire. He started crying. It was his Dad's new, never-been-used fishing rod, taken without permission.

"Dad's gonna kill me. He saved all winter to get this pole." He kept on crying. We tried to console him, but to no avail. As Arnold and I crawled into our sleeping bags we giggled, of all the luck Butch Tilton had the worst. It was about two in the morning when I awoke. I crawled out of the tent and stepped into the darkness to relieve myself. When I returned I threw two more logs on the dim fire and noticed that Perry was curled around the glowing coals. I crawled into our tent and then noticed the bright glow of the fresh fire. I looked toward Perry. His sleeping bag was smoking. "Hey, Perry."

"Yeah, Vince."

"You're sleeping bag's on fire."

"Good, thanks, g'night."

I woke Arnold, and he raised up on his elbow.

"Watch this Arnie, it's gonna be good."

Arnie wiped the sleep from his eyes and grinned as he saw the end of Perry's sleeping bag smoking. Suddenly Perry let out a scream and kicked wildly. He looked like a huge inchworm. He couldn't get his bag unzipped and he rolled over and over, screaming and yelling as flames flickered. Arnold scampered from the tent and poured water from his canteen on the flames. Smoke rose and everyone laughed, but Perry got mad at Arnold for pouring water on his new sleeping bag. That ticked Arnie off and he threw his empty canteen at the frowning inchworm.

"Dumb son of a . . . , I should have let him burn up," he said. I laughed and slapped him on the back as he crawled back into his sleeping bag. Meanwhile Perry was stomping around the fire, still mad about getting his feet wet. I smiled and closed my eyes, dawn would soon arrive. I awoke to the smell of coffee. We sat around drinking coffee for a while until Bill Decker came running up. "Hey guys, I found an old grave by a stream." We all jumped up and followed him through the brush to the small stone about a hundred yards from camp. It read "Henry White, 1876–1922, R.I.P."

Bill had dropped to his knees to clean and then read the inscription. As he knelt the temptation was too great for Perry. He reached out and knocked off Bill's new straw hat. We all laughed and Bill stood, his face turning red. Perry laughed and pointed at the hat. Then Bill took a step and reached up and removed Perry's prize derby. We all looked at each other and Arnie whispered in my ear, "Boy, this is gonna be good." Bill gently placed the derby on the ground. He looked up at Perry and paused for a moment. Then in a flash he raised his right foot and stomped the derby flat. Perry's mouth flew open and he shook with rage. He stood silently not moving. Bill folded his arms and smiled at Perry. All was still for a few seconds, then Perry reached down and picked up Bill's straw hat. He pulled his knife from its scabbard and cut the top off Bill's new hat. He put the knife back in his scabbard and then with both hands he placed the straw hat back on Bill's head. Bill's eyes bugged and his mouth was twisted. Like two mountain rams the two boys lunged at each other and the fists flew. Don started to break up the fight, but I stopped him. "Let 'em fight, Don, this thing's been festering for a long time." He thought a moment, "Yeah, you're right." Just about that time we both winced as Bill caught Perry square in the mouth with an overhand right, knocking him to the ground. Instead of jumping on him the smaller Bill yelled, "Get up ya big jerk!" Perry jumped up and kicked Bill right between the legs. Bill dropped straight down on his knees holding his privates, then Perry hit him hard across the face and Bill fell face down in the mud. Perry started to go after Bill again, but Steve and Butch stopped him. Perry breathed deeply. This was probably the only fight he had ever won in his life.

"It's over," Don yelled, as Bill held his jaw and spit blood. Perry reached down to help Bill up and Bill knocked his hand away. He stood without help. Perry stuck his hand out to shake hands and Bill paused for a second. Then he too stuck out his hand and the two enemies shook hands. Slowly smiles came to their faces and by the time we reached camp they were laughing and joking with each other. We broke camp around noon and Don's parents picked us up and brought us back to Tulsa. The next day at school we heard that Butch was grounded for the rest of his life. That was our last outing together. High school was on the horizon, and a place called Vietnam was beginning to make news.

FIVE // **The Last Mariachi**

In June 1963 Uncle Claude was on his way over to our house to deliver our new mariachi suits. Uncle Claude took our measurements in March, then drove to Guadalajara, Mexico, to have them made. Now they would soon be here. I listened as Dad played his soprano saxophone. He was a true master, he loved to play his music. He always called it his music and it was. He would blow into his soprano sax and from it would come forth a tone never heard before, mellow and sweet. I had heard other musicians try to play the soprano sax; they were terrible, they sounded like a party horn or tin can. They didn't have what Dad had, the love of music, and the love of his saxophone. He would sit for hours and play, reveling in his world of sharps and flats. His eyes would take on a faraway look as he played his sweet music. For the length of a song he would be transported back in time. Perhaps he was thinking of his father, who had died in his arms when Dad was nineteen, or perhaps he was playing a fiesta during the Depression years. No one knew what the master was thinking as he played his songs. He would play "Sin Ti" at the Mexican dances and you could hear the people swoon. The Mexican colonia in Tulsa had what no other colonia in the world could have, Concho Mendoza and his sweet music.

There was a knock at the door and the sweet melody of "Adios Mi Chaparrita" came to an abrupt halt as Dad lowered his saxophone and stood to answer the door. Uncle Claude entered, a large box under under his left arm and in his right hand a quart bottle of Falstaff beer. "Here, Banson," he said as he turned sideways and I took the large box from him. He set his beer down and opened the box. He reached inside it, stopped and looked up at me and Dad, then smiled. Slowly he pulled a mariachi jacket from the box. It was gray, with black designs embroidered on the back and arms and front. It was beautiful. Then he pulled the pants from the box and they had embroidered black designs down each leg. They looked sharp. Dad and I smiled at each other. As Claude handed me my jacket he got a somber look on his face. He looked into my eyes, "Banson, you are the last mariachi." Dad and Claude looked at each other and I knew they were thinking of their past. Dad put his hand on my back, "Son, there will be no more mariachis from the Mendoza family. You are the last. I want you to know that I'm proud of you." All I could manage was a "Thanks, Dad." Then Uncle Claude handed Dad his suit, and we both tried on our new jackets. They were a perfect fit. Dad and Claude took turns drinking Uncle Claude's beer while they discussed what to wear with the outfits. Finally Mom stepped in with her two cents worth, and Uncle Claude and Dad agreed. We would wear red ties, red cumberbunds and black Mexican-style boots.

A month later we were on our way to play a dance in Omaha, Nebraska. It was summer and the drive was long and hot. As we entered Nebraska I could not believe the amount of corn that stretched before my eyes. Row after row of it, as far as the eye could see. It boggled my mind to see such an expanse. Near evening we passed by the stockyards on our way into Omaha. "Dad! Stop it!" I yelled, as the stench of the stockyard filled my nostrils. I covered my face with a pillow, and Mom and Dad laughed. Uncle Claude, with Aunt Julia and Cousin Ray, proudly drove his new Mercury through downtown Omaha. We followed in our 1955 yellow and white Chevrolet sedan. Behind us came Lucille and Charlie Mendoza, and riding with them was Victor Mendoza. We stopped in front of a small Mexican restaurant. It was in an old part of Omaha, everything needed painting. We followed Uncle Claude into the restaurant. To his surprise no one knew who we were. Then he explained to the owner, Señor Ortiz, that we were to meet Señor José Gomez at the restaurant. Mr. Ortiz smiled and said he would contact Señor Gomez. He then invited us to eat. Later Señor Gomez arrived, he was short and thin with gray hair. He and Uncle Claude talked for a while in Spanish, and after Señor Gomez left, Uncle Claude told us that he had all the directions to our motel and the dance hall. Everything was taken care of.

At eight o'clock that evening we entered the large dance hall. We set up the amplifiers and microphones, then we tested them for feedback. Everything was all set for the dance. We stepped offstage and walked to a large room. Several Mexican men from Omaha were there and they served us mixed drinks. Much to my surprise Dad handed me a cup of bourbon and Coke. I took a swallow. As the alcohol took my breath away I gasped for air and the rest of the band laughed at the expression on my face. They really laughed when I said that the drink was good. I had never really thought about drinking. Oh, I'd seen my Dad drink when he played music, and he might have a beer when he and I watched baseball on television, but he was no alcoholic or anything like that, and so I drank the mixed drink. I figured it was part of growing up.

Uncle Claude was talking rather loudly with Señor Gomez. I saw Señor Gomez pleading with Uncle Claude, then Uncle Claude walked away and made his way over to Dad and me.

"They don't have the money to pay us, so I told them that we wouldn't go on until they pay us cash up front," he said.

Dad and I nodded our heads in agreement. Señor Gomez and the other Mexican men from Omaha talked rapidly in Spanish, then seven men quickly left the room. It was twenty minutes until the dance was to begin, and I casually walked to the stage and peered out from behind the curtain. People were already beginning to filter in and I was surprised that there were Mexicans as far north as Nebraska. The twenty minutes passed and there was still no sign of Señor Gomez. We could hear the audience talking and it sounded like bees buzzing. At nine-fifteen Señor Gomez entered with a fistful of money. He and Uncle Claude quickly counted it, then shook hands and Uncle Claude stuffed the money in his front pocket. "Show time! Let's go!" We quickly hurried onstage. The instruments had already been tuned, but Dad and the others checked them again quickly and we were set. Uncle Claude nodded his head and the curtains rose as we played the Mendoza theme song, "Las Altanitas."

The dance went smoothly. Señor Gomez asked Victor to perform a couple of songs during the intermission and Victor asked me if I would accompany him. I was glad to, in fact I was honored. After the dance we returned to our motel room, it had been a long day.

The next morning we were up ten o'clock and on the road shortly after. The morning was bright and sunny as we sped along the gray ribbon of highway. At noon Uncle Claude stopped in a small town for lunch. It was a clean-looking little town, much like the small towns back home. The restaurant was on the main street. It had a lot of big windows in the front. We waited for the others to park and then we entered the restaurant as a group. We seated ourselves at two large booths and talked and laughed as we waited to place our order. Ten minutes passed and still no waitress. Fifteen minutes passed and Charlie asked for some service from the waitress who stood behind the counter.

"Sorry, but we don't serve Indians in this restaurant," she said, chewing her gum and nervously twitching the pencil in her hand. There was absolute silence as all the white people in the restaurant stared at us.

"Oh, we're not Indians, we're Mexicans," Charlie said smiling.

"That's worse," the little blonde waitress said. "I'm gonna have to ask you to leave."

I will never forget the look on Charlie and Lucille's faces. They looked so hurt. They timidly stood with the others and slowly walked to the door.

"Mama, they can't do that," I said. I was mad, as the white people continued to stare.

"Banson, it's okay," Uncle Claude said.

"No it's not," I said, stopping and looking defiantly toward the restaurant. Mama pulled me by my arm, "C'mon, get in the car."

I couldn't believe what had happened. I didn't feel hurt, I felt mad. I could see why the coloreds acted like they did. I could see why they wanted equality. I didn't like being treated like dirt. So what if we were Indians, so what if we were Mexicans. We are Americans! One of my uncles, who was almost full-blood Creek, died in Italy protecting his country. My other Indian uncles served in the war also. Mexican Americans had won more medals of honor than any other ethnic group during World War II, yet these yokels in Nebraska had the gall to run us out of their restaurant. We didn't stop to eat until we reached Kansas, but the bitterness still festered inside me. We got home late that evening.

We played a lot of dances that summer. We played in Oklahoma City for the Mexican colonia. We also played around Tulsa, at the Moose lodge and the Blue Moon, which was on North Cincinnati, and at private parties for the rich oil men. But my favorite dance hall was the VFW hall on Sixth Street in Tulsa. I had my favorite songs also: "Torero," "Soy Mexicano", and "Jesusita en Chihuahua."

My favorite couple was Joe and Virginia Rodrigues. They were about the same age as my parents. Virginia was white, she was dark-haired and pretty. She must have been a saint to put up with Joe. He was a character, talked loud and always had a drink in his hand at the dances. He always pestered Dad and the rest of the band to play "Mi Ranchito," his favorite song. We all liked him. He was really a good man and a leader in the Mexican colonia in Tulsa. Joe was crippled, his right hand and wrist were impaired and also his right leg. He had been severely wounded during the Battle of the Bulge. It was bitterly cold, and Joe and his buddy crawled across the open, snow-covered land toward the woods in search of fuel. They gathered an armful of wood, then started crawling back across the open ground toward their lines. It was then that the Germans saw them and opened up with machine guns. The burst of fire killed Joe's buddy and badly wounded Joe. He lay out in the open for hours as the fighting continued. He prayed and promised God that if he lived through this ordeal he would serve the church until his dying day. Bravery was in Joe's blood. His father, Rufino, had saved one hundred ninety men in a coal mine disaster in 1912 at Lehigh's number five mine in Oklahoma. For his heroism Rufino received a bronze medal from the Carnegie Hero Fund Commission. And Joe, being a man of his word, gave generously to the Catholic Church throughout the remainder of his life.

It was a sunny morning as Arnold and I waited for the bus at the corner of Waco and Easton. It was the first day of school, and we were off once again on a new adventure . . . high school. Central High was located in downtown Tulsa. Arnold and I watched as the city bus came to a stop in front of us, the smell of diesel filled the air, and the door slid open before us. We paid our money, then looked for a place to sit down. Ha! No way. Arnold and I looked at each other and shook our heads as the bus lurched forward and we grabbed for the overhead rail. Two blocks later the bus stopped again to pick up more members of the future of America. I looked at Arnold and he had a frown on his face.

"What's wrong, Arnie?"

"This guy over here smells like a bear."

I laughed out loud and Arnie told me to shut up, and I laughed even harder. The bus let us off at the First Baptist Church, directly across the street from the bus station, and we walked the remaining two blocks to Central. The school didn't seem too large until you got inside, then it seemed huge. We went in the main entrance. Before us was a large stairway. We climbed the stairs, class schedule in hand, and as we reached the top of the stairs we saw it, the large bronze sculpture titled "The Great Spirit." The sculpture was beautiful. The Indian sat atop his horse, he wore only a warbonnet and loincloth. His hands were extended to the side, palms up, and his face looked upward toward the heavens. We stared at the work of art until we noticed that other students who had to be juniors or seniors were giving us funny looks and we realized that we were acting like sophomores. Arnie and I quickly said our goodbyes and left in opposite directions.

I had the usual classes, math, history, English, Spanish, band, and gym. Sixth-hour gym was a special class for jocks only and I felt proud to be included. Math, history, and English bored me. I looked forward to playing in the band. I was seated in the saxophone section next to a girl. I had never seen a girl with such an interesting face. She had dishwater blonde hair, green eyes, and pretty teeth. Her lips were thin and her nose turned up just enough to be cute. As I sat down next to her, I looked her over.

"Hi, my name's Vince," I said smiling.

"My name's Lola. I saw you looking at me. Don't you go getting any ideas! I know your type! Shame on you!"

My mouth flew open. Jeez! I had only introduced myself. She turned her head away from me, but I could tell from the side of her face that she was smiling. I knew in an instant that I had a game player on my hands. She turned her head to look at me.

"Are you someone's mother?" I asked, and she almost laughed out loud. Then to my surprise she started talking in a southern accent. I was never bored seated next to Lola. She was a junior and according to school etiquette she could never, ever go out with a sophomore. She did try to talk me into joining the marching band next year, however. She also said it was possible for people to cuddle and snuggle in the back of the bus during the long out-of-town trips that the band took with the football team. I knew she was playing with me so I decided to play into her hands. "You know you're driving me crazy," I said softly. A sneaky little smile crossed her lips as she looked at me, then she ignored me during the rest of the class. I was dying laughing on the inside. I would glance at her out of the corner of my eye, she would be doing the same toward me. Every day for one hour we would toy with each other much like a soap opera, it was a year of fun with Lola.

Despite the embarrassment, Spanish class was fun too. Arnold and I sat next to each other, which didn't help. We were known as "No es correcto," for each time Arnold or I would answer a question from Mrs. Potter, she would immediately say, "No es correcto." By the third week of class when either of us answered, Mrs. Potter, like an orchestra conductor, would raise both arms toward the sky and the entire class would say, "No es correcto!" We would laugh with the other students and sit back down. There was one girl that had just moved from Alabama. She amazed me. I had never heard Spanish spoken with a southern accent. She kept the class and Mrs. Potter in stitches. Instead of saying, "Sí, sí, señor," Lou Ann would say, "See-ya, see-ya, sen-yo-wah." And the class would die laughing!

I had fun in Spanish class, but there is one reason why I'll never forget it. It was in Spanish class that we heard the announcement that President Kennedy had been assassinated. I was shocked and hurt like the rest of the world. I felt as if I had lost a part of my own family. I liked the man, he had courage and wisdom. Now he was gone forever, the world would never be the same. As I watched the riderless horse being led in the funeral procession I wondered what kind of a world this was, where the president of the United States could get slaughtered in one of the largest cities in America. Corruptness flourished and decency and honesty would soon be a thing of the past, just like the buffalo.

I went to gym class but I felt like an impostor. I was no athlete. I was average. I watched as lesser boys, in my eye, made the football team. I was filled with jealousy and despair. I ran with the cross-country team, but I never actually made the team. I was a "wanna-be." No longer could I run for miles feeling the wind in my hair and never getting tired. I labored to run five miles when the other boys I had beaten easily before my accident were running ten miles a night.

My junior year arrived, and I readied myself for a boring year. I was pretty much a loner. I still saw Arnie now and then, but he had made the basketball team and spent most of his time shooting baskets. My other friends were athletes, and though I saw them in sixth-hour gym I was just a face in the crowd. My grades were average, and if I had studied I'm sure that they would have improved, but I was satisfied with getting by. I walked the halls in my own little world. I had been pretty popular with my friends in junior high, but here at Central the story was different. There were over eight hundred kids at this school, and I rarely saw my old friends. I did see Chrissy one day. She was walking with her latest beau. His father was an attorney, and her beau drove a new sports car. I smiled to myself as she looked at me, then she quickly looked away. There were several pretty girls at Central, but I never tried to date them. I guess I felt like I didn't have anything to offer them, since I couldn't be active in sports. So I remained quiet and alone until I met Bonnie. Bonnie was a pretty girl with long dark brown hair and the prettiest brown eyes I had ever seen. She was white, but I never thought of race being a problem. She was in my homeroom, and like me she was quiet. We met by accident.

Our homeroom class was English. We were to read a book and then give a report on it. Scholar that I was, I briefly skimmed through the book the night before our report was due. The next day in class my name was called and I slowly walked to the front of the room. I smiled at Mrs. Dickinson, and she looked at me coldly. I took my place behind the podium and cleared my throat as my mind frantically raced in search of a plot. "The name of my book is . . . The name of my book." My God, I had forgotten the name of the book! I turned toward Mrs. Dickinson, "Excuse me," I said, then I walked to my desk and looked at the book. Quickly I returned to the podium as my classmates laughed. I smiled at Mrs. Dickinson, who was staring daggers at me, I was glad she didn't have a gun. I continued with what I thought was a very interesting story. My classmates smiled as I rambled on about tigers and pirates, race cars and saloons. Ha! I was a literary genius, and my classmates applauded at my wit. Mrs. Dickinson, told me through clenched teeth to take my seat. She walked to the podium and looked directly at me as she spoke.

"Mr. Mendoza, I too have read *Where the Red Fern Grows*. I do not recall tigers, pirates, or saloons. I'm sure that you will better interpret this book during summer school." The class let out a low moan as Mrs. Dickinson drove home her point. She called on Sally who sat behind me for the next report. The poor girl was so nervous that her voice shook; it sounded half human and half goat and everyone smiled at her misfortune. After class I was standing out in the hallway consoling her. She was a nice girl, with brown hair and freckles. She had a great personality and we became good friends. Then Bonnie appeared at our side.

"Vince, can I talk to you?"

"Sure," I said. Sally and I said our goodbyes, and she was off to her next class. I looked at Bonnie and smiled. She was pretty, and I wondered why I hadn't noticed her before. She was short, with a perfect figure. She had a pretty smile. "I liked your story," she said smiling. I laughed aloud, "Yeah, I did too."

"I especially liked the part where the pirates jumped in their race cars to get away from the tigers, then stopped in the saloon and got into a fight with a bunch of off-duty cops." She started laughing again. "Cathy and I were laughing so hard that we started crying," she said as she looked up at me.

"Where's your next class?" I asked.

"It's up on three."

"My class is on one, but I'll walk you to the stairs,"

"I'd like that," she said smiling.

I saw her at school for two weeks. I walked her here and there, then we'd meet for lunch, finally I asked her out on a date. It was Friday night and I stopped my 1958 two-tone green Pontiac Starchief in front of her house on South Trenton. I walked up the driveway and onto the long porch. I knocked on the door and waited. Soon a little gray-haired lady answered the door and I asked for Bonnie. Mrs. Hall invited me in and I stood waiting for Bonnie to appear. Mrs. Hall and I chatted for a while. She seemed nice, and I felt at ease with her. Suddenly Bonnie appeared, she looked great. She wore a white blouse, black slacks, and black pumps, and across her arm she carried a black sweater. We said our good-byes, with me promising to have her home before midnight.

We drove to the Admiral Twin Drive-in. A James Bond movie was playing and we quickly made a run to the concession stand and then returned to the privacy of my car. We laughed and talked and she told me about her family and I told her of mine. She was pretty and sweet, and I really liked her, but I wasn't crazy in love. About halfway through the movie I put my arm around her and she snuggled in close. She rested her head on my shoulder and as I looked into her eyes my heart rate quickened. She partially closed her eyes and parted her lips. I ever so slightly moved my lips closer and closer until they were but a breath away, then softly I kissed her full on the mouth. All of my burners ignited, but I had them under control. I was cool, I was macho, I was home free.

It was about this time in my life that Cousin Ray Mendoza wanted to establish a band of his own. Uncle Claude let Ray play his guitar occasionally at the Mexican dances, but Ray wanted more and he asked me if I would be interested in starting a band with him. I eagerly said yes, and within the week he had a practice set up. Ray, who was older than I, played rhythm guitar and sang. I played the tenor sax, Jim Carter played bass, Joe Morrison played lead guitar, and Larry Grimes played drums. Ray named us "The Jalapeños." We played Mexican and country western music and everything that Tony Orlando and Trini Lopez recorded. Our first dance was held at the VFW hall and I was pretty nervous. Here I was the son of the best sax player in the Midwest and everyone was eager to see if I could hold my own with the master. I didn't know if Ray was nervous or not, if he was he didn't show it. Everything went smoothly and we were successful at our first dance, and Ray was on cloud nine. Ray and his pretty wife, Virginia, treated the band to breakfast at one of the all-night restaurants. We played well and throughout high school I made some pretty good money by playing in both bands.

It was December when Mama got the call. Grandpa McIntosh had had a stroke. Mama made me go to school the next day, but she and Dad drove to Okmulgee that night. Grandpa stayed bedridden until he passed away in January 1965. Before the service for Grandpa I followed Grandma, Mama, and Aunt Lucy to the small white church where Grandpa lay. As I entered the church I couldn't believe my eyes, Grandma was standing beside Grandpa's casket and Aunt Lucy was taking a snapshot. She took a few more pictures and then they stood and talked awhile. I was horrified. I had never seen anyone take pictures of a dead person. I stood away from the casket and looked at my Grandpa. I couldn't cry. Grandpa had never been a part of me. He'd ignored me at best, almost as if he hated me. I stood staring at his old body, and inside I felt as if he were a stranger. I asked Grandma why she had taken pictures of Grandpa in the casket. She looked at me and smiled. "Vincent, Preacher and I had pictures taken together as man and wife." I nodded my head. "I lived my whole life with that man, I never knew any other. I don't see nothing wrong with taking pictures now that he has left me. This is a part of my life, and I want a photo of him in death, because it is a part of my life."

I accepted Grandma's logic and respected her for it. I felt sorry for my grandmother for losing Grandpa, but Grandma was tough and she handled his passing well.

SIX // **Girls, Girls, Girls**

It was spring of 1965 when Wayne Hamilton and I set off on a double date with a couple of sisters from Mounds, Oklahoma. I liked Wayne. He was a senior at Central and he and I got along great. He had brown hair and sported a flattop haircut. We sped down Highway 75, as the sun sank low on the horizon. Soon we pulled into the driveway of the small country home. Wayne drove through some feeding chickens, scattering them in all directions as the gray 1952 Plymouth coupe slid to a stop in front of the white farmhouse.

"Now remember I get the prettiest one," he said.

"Yeah, I know it's your car and your booze, so you get the pick of the litter," I said, acting disappointed. Wayne laughed and knocked on the door. Soon we were driving down a country road with the two pretty sisters. This was my first blind date, and I missed the closeness of Bonnie. I had only come along to help out Wayne, and now I was sitting next to a fourteen-year-old girl . . . good grief! We pulled off the dirt road and drove across a pasture to a tree line. Wayne parked the car and Amy and I took a blanket and pillow and walked toward a large tree. Wayne and Becky stayed in the car. I opened two bottles of Lonestar beer as we sat cross-legged on the blanket, her knee touching mine. "You're Indian, ain't ya?" Amy asked.

"Yep, my Dad's Mexican and Mom's Creek."

"I know a lot of Creek boys from Okmulgee," she said, "but I ain't never kissed one."

There it was, the opening line to love, I thought. I leaned over to kiss her and she pushed me away, then muttered something about not being in the mood. She jumped up and walked into the darkness. Shoot! At least I had my beer, so I took a chug and just about that time she screamed and came running to me out of the darkness.

I was halfway standing when she plowed into me sending us both head over heels. As we looked up we saw a light coming through the woods and we realized that they were coon hunters and that what she had heard was more than likely the coon. Just then Wayne and Becky emerged from the car, and we talked and passed the beer around. We drove in to Okmulgee for a hamburger and then pulled back out onto Highway 75, singing "She Loves You" with the Beatles. Wayne and I didn't get back to Tulsa until daybreak. Luckily, my folks were still asleep as I crawled through my bedroom window. I slept well that day.

The next week I kept getting phone calls from the popular kids at Central. Of course most of them I knew from junior high. They wanted me to join a boys' club made up of the most popular boys from each high school in town. The club was called Tops. Time after time I declined their invitation, and it seemed like each time they phoned, my Dad was always near the phone. One day he asked me why they wanted me to join their club, and I told him. I couldn't believe that he actually got mad. "You stay with your own kind! You're not white! You'll never be white! You don't belong with those white boys! You're Mexican and Indian, stay in your place and forget about being white!" I couldn't believe my ears. He and Mom had moved me out of the Mexican neighborhood that I loved. It was Mom who wouldn't let me go to the Indian school in Tahlequah. They didn't want me to be white, Mexican, or Indian. I was totally lost as to who I was.

Things got worse as summer arrived. I pulled up in front of Bonnie's house. Before I could get out of the car I saw Bonnie walking quickly toward me. She opened the door and got in.

"Let's go Vince, hurry."

I stepped on the accelerator and sped off as she wiped the tears from her eyes.

"I hate him," she said.

"Hate who? What's going on?"

"My father. He doesn't want me to see you any longer."

"Why? What did I do?"

"You're Mexican. He hates you because you're Mexican."

I drove to a nearby park and stopped the car.

"Bonnie, this isn't something that I can just turn off."

"I feel the same way, Vince, he's not going to stop us. I'll sneak around if I have to. From now on pick me up at my girlfriend's house," she scribbled an address on a piece of paper and handed it to me. "I love you, Vince. Next year when we're away at college he won't be able to do anything about us." We kissed and I cursed myself for being different. As I looked at her I had already made my mind up. If this didn't go well I would set her free. There was no use in making her suffer because of me, only time would tell.

A month later I was on my way to another Mexican dance, but this time I wasn't going to play. I had decided that I would sit this one out and enjoy myself. It was at the VFW hall again and as I joined a table of friends I happened to look up at the entrance to the dance hall. There stood the prettiest girl I had ever seen. She was blonde. She wore a tight black dress with matching high heels and rhinestone earrings and necklace. I stood mesmerized. It was then that I realized that she was with my cousin Tony, who was five years younger than me. I walked toward them and then I saw the Flores family, Albert, Martha, J. R., Mickey, Teresa, and little Andy. They were all together and as I said hello I discovered that this girl was a friend of Teresa's. We all walked to an empty table and I sat with them, never taking my eyes off the beautiful creature in front of me. Not wanting to seem too eager I didn't ask her to dance right away. I stared at her well-developed body and watched her beautiful face as she danced with Tony. This is what it was all about, man and woman, yin and yang, George and Gracie . . . this was it! I asked her to dance when I recognized the melody of a song, a bolero called "Green Eyes." She smiled as I slipped my arm around her waist, she felt good in my arms. We talked as we danced, her name was Debbie, she went to Charles Page High School in Sand Springs, Oklahoma, which was just a few miles from where I lived.

"You're the prettiest girl I've ever seen," I said, looking into her beautiful face. She smiled and thanked me for the compliment.

"I'm going to marry you," I said, and she laughed. "No, I really am," I said.

"What makes you think I'd marry you?" she asked, still smiling.

"Well, first of all I'm cute, plus I've got a lot of potential, and most important I'd never look at another woman as long as I had you."

She continued smiling, "Well I'm sorry, but you're too late, I'm already engaged."

"What?"

"I'm engaged to a captain in the army. I'm going to be an officer's wife."

The smile left my face. "Why would a captain in the army want to marry you? Can't he get a woman his own age? He must be a reject."

"He is not a reject, he's a very handsome man."

Just then the song ended and I walked her back to our table. We all had a good time dancing and it was fun. As the last song of the evening was played I danced with Debbie again.

"Can I call you tomorrow?" I asked.

"No, Vincent, I'm engaged. I'm promised to someone else, I'm sorry."

"You're not as sorry as I am." The song ended and I walked her to her friends who waited at the table for her. We said good-bye and I stood there as she walked away. She stopped at the doorway and turned to look at me, then blew me a kiss. I slowly saluted her and she smiled, then turned and walked away. My God, she was pretty, I thought, that old captain was a lucky man. I sighed deeply as I stood there until I heard my Dad call my name, and then I hurried to the bandstand to help break down the equipment.

It was Friday afternoon and Mom had just arrived home from work. She worked at the Zebco plant in Tulsa along with Aunt Connie and Lucille Mendoza. Every Friday after work she would stop and buy groceries. I always helped carry in the precious cargo. It was a good time in my life, and as I carried bag after bag of groceries into our house on West Brady I looked forward to our Friday routine. Mom would cook hamburgers while Dad and I watched Walter Cronkite on the evening news and recent film footage of U.S. Marines in combat in Vietnam. I'd watch as boys carried their wounded to a waiting helicopter, and I wondered why the United States always had to send our guys into foreign conflict. What was wrong with the rest of the world? Then we'd watch *Rawhide*, there was a new cowboy on television, Clint Eastwood. He was pretty good, but he wasn't John Wayne by any means. Sometimes we'd watch *Combat*, then after it was over I'd get ready to go on a date if Bonnie could get away. If she was busy I'd go over to a friend's house and play poker. It was a simple routine, and I loved it. I had just finished combing my hair when the phone rang. Dad was in the toilet, which was a danger zone for at least an hour after he left, and Mom was over at Linda's house. I hurried to the phone. It was my cousin Butch.

"How's it goin, cuz?" Butch asked.

"Fair to middling, how about you?"

"I'm quitting school, cuz. I'm joining the Marines."

"Quitting school? Are you crazy? Why?"

"I'm just tired of it, man. I'm not getting anywhere."

"C'mon Butch, give it one more year."

"No, I've thought it out. Besides, I've already signed up. Is Aunt Martha there?"

"Naw, she's over at Linda's house."

"Well, tell her I called. I'll be seeing you."

"Keep your chebo down," I said with a laugh.

"You bet, catch ya later, cuz." He hung up the phone and he was gone. I couldn't believe that he'd do such a stupid thing. Butch was smart, at least I'd thought he was until he called, and he was tough. This joining the Marine Corps caught me completely off guard. I stood there thinking, why?

Later that night Wayne and I were at a Tulsa Oilers baseball game. We sat up high in the old wooden stadium. Many concession stands were located behind us on the upper level, the yellow lights gave everything a yellow glow, and the smell of cigar smoke filled the air. I told Wayne about Butch joining the Marine Corps. Wayne looked at me with an odd expression on his face. "What's wrong with that?" He said.

"What's wrong with that! They're killing people over there. I'm not getting my butt shot off in some foreign country. I don't even know where Vietnam is!"

"Vince, I've already signed up."

"You what? Wait a minute, Wayne, I thought we were going to college at Northeastern State together. Remember? I graduate next year and by the time I get there you already have everything checked out. You know, the panty raids and all that stuff!" Wayne just looked away.

"Vince, man, this is something I just gotta do."

"Don't be stupid!" I said, and Wayne got mad. I didn't press it any further. Wayne dropped me off in front of my house after the game and as he drove away into the darkness I couldn't help wondering what had happened to my friend. Why had he suddenly changed his mind? I mean it's a free country and all, but why the Marines? Vietnam was out there somewhere. Life would be so much nicer in Tahlequah. I shrugged my shoulders and walked up the steep driveway. The lights had been left on for me and as I entered the house I yelled out, "Mom, I'm home!"

"Turn out the light, baby," she yelled back.

"Yeah, like I'm some kind of moron," I muttered.

"What?"

"Love you," I said. "God, she still calls me baby," I added under my breath. I walked the darkened hallway to my room.

Two days passed and as I got home from school the phone rang. It was Wayne. "Hey, Vince, I'll be over in five minutes."

Five minutes later Wayne was walking through my front door. He wore penny loafers, wheat jeans, and a red V-neck sweater. He plopped down in Dad's worn green recliner and lit a cigarette.

"Remember the other night at the ballgame?"

I nodded to Wayne, as he took a drag off the cigarette in his hand.

"Ya see, I do want to go to school, but I want to get this service thing out of the way. I don't want to have to keep looking over my shoulder every time I take an exam. If you flunk out your ass gets drafted. I'd rather enlist and be a U.S. Marine. I'd hate to get drafted by the air force. I mean who wants to walk around airports looking like a dang bus driver! And another thing, if I did get in the war I'd rather have a real bus driver beside me, ya get my drift?"

"Yeah, I gotcha."

"Good, let's eat," Wayne said. He sprang out of Dad's chair and headed for the kitchen.

It was a bright sunny Saturday morning and I was outside washing my car. Two weeks had passed since I had last seen Wayne. I figured he was taking care of his personal matters before leaving for the Marines. Suddenly Mom yelled out the back door that I had a phone call. I hurried inside thinking that it might be Bonnie, but it wasn't.

"Vince, how ya doing, partner?" Wayne asked.

"Man, where have you been?"

"Vince, I've met the greatest girl in the world. I think I'm in love. She's got it all."

"Again," I said.

"No, really, I think I am. Listen, we're having a party tonight, can you make it?"

"Sure, Wayne, where is it gonna be?"

"Over at Carter's house. His parents are gone for the weekend."

"Great, see ya tonight."

I arrived at seven o'clock that evening. Donnie Carter and Diane

James were sitting on the front porch drinking beer. She was a cute little blonde and Donnie was a redhead with freckles. He was on the chunky side and he was always getting grounded, more than likely he would be grounded for this party too. I made my way to the kitchen and got myself a cold one and a sandwich. There was a poker game going on in the back bedroom. The other bedroom door was locked, so I could imagine what was going on in there. I had just stepped into the dining room when someone grabbed me and turned me around. The next thing I knew Glenda was kissing me.

Glenda was what we called in our neighborhood "a good old girl." I'd had my chance with Glenda at the swimming pool when I was twelve, and ever since then she had ignored me until now. She was still very pretty, athletically slim, with long curly brown hair, blue eyes, and long legs. Lots of guys wanted Glenda for their steady, but Glenda was a free spirit. She wanted a lot of boyfriends and believe me she had a lot of boyfriends. I was sure that when I was old and gray and sitting in a rundown nursing home, Glenda Miles would cross my mind and she would still be nineteen and beautiful.

At eight o'clock I heard Wayne's "ahoogah" horn blowing and his motor revving. I made my way to the front porch and saw Wayne pulling a wheelchair from the trunk of his car. This has got to be a joke, I thought. Then I looked at the girl in the front seat, it was no joke. The girl was Leslie Glenn. She was a handicapped girl from Central. I had always felt uneasy around handicapped people, and I'd never met anyone confined to a chair. Then I remembered what Wayne had said about her, so I ran to the kitchen and grabbed two beers and headed back to Wayne's car. By the time I got there, Leslie was already in the chair. "Here you go, good-looking!" I said and handed her a beer.

"Thanks, Vince," she said, giving me a big smile.

"Have we met?" I asked.

"No, but all the girls know you," she said still smiling.

I blushed when she said that, and she laughed out loud.

"Well, everyone knows me too, but only as the girl in the wheelchair, right?"

"Well, yeah," I said feeling embarrassed and blushing again.

She gave me a wink and took a long drink of her beer. Wayne and I lifted her in her chair onto the porch and wheeled her into the middle of the party. She was cute, with a little pixie face, black hair, and blue eyes. I couldn't believe how much spirit and confidence she had. She and Wayne made quite a pair. She wore light green slacks and a sheer white blouse. Her shoes were black-and-white oxfords. She was everything Wayne had said about her. I didn't feel the least bit uncomfortable around her and I told her so. Later we talked and she told me she and Wayne planned to be married as soon as he returned from overseas. I was happy for them. Wayne had found himself a real prize. "Honey, time to go," Wayne said as he stepped out onto the porch.

"All right, let me get one more beer for the road," she said.

"You keep drinking that beer and I'm gonna have to set you on a five-gallon bucket so I won't have to lift you out to pee."

Leslie turned to look at me, then shook her head and smiled. As they rounded the corner in Wayne's old car I smiled too, they were good for each other. Then I thought of Glenda and I trotted back to the party.

It was Monday morning and I met Bonnie before class at "The Great Spirit."

"Vince, I don't know what to do."

"What's wrong, baby?"

"It's Dad, he's gone crazy. All he does is harp on me about seeing you."

"How about if I talk to him."

"Oh God, no. I don't know what he'd do, Vince, he's bonkers."

"Let's cool it for a couple of weeks, Bonnie."

"I don't want to, Vince. I don't want to lose you because of him."

"It's only two weeks, besides you don't need to be put through any more than you already have. We can still see each other at school."

"Well, okay, but in two weeks we're going out."

"That's a date," I said as I kissed her lightly and she giggled.

That afternoon when I arrived home from school I checked the mailbox as I always did. We had the usual bills and junk mail. A yellow piece of paper from the post office said there was a certified letter for Dad that he needed to pick up. I laid all the mail on the dining room table and went on my way. The next afternoon as I watched television I heard Dad pull into our driveway and slam the car door as usual and soon I heard his footsteps on the porch. He opened the front door and walked in.

He stood there glaring at me, waving a letter in his hand. "I want you to stop seeing Bonnie!" he yelled, as he set his gray lunch pail down on the coffee table. I was caught by complete surprise.

"What? What do you mean?"

"I got this letter from Mr. Hall. He wants you to stop seeing Bonnie or he's going to file harassment charges against you."

"Harassment? Hell he's harassing me, Dad!"

"Don't you talk to me like that, it's over. You stop seeing her! Ay no mas!"

I was fuming. "Mr. Hall, you old S.O.B.," I muttered.

Later that night I talked to Mom and she sided with Dad. We didn't need any trouble, she told me; even though she liked Bonnie she wanted me to stop seeing her. Two weeks passed slowly. Friday morning Bonnie was all smiles, "Tonight's the night! Oh, Vince, I can hardly wait, I've missed you so much," she cooed. "Pick me up at the corner at eight o'clock, that way they won't see me leave."

"Sure, Bonnie, whatever you say, babe."

Later that evening as I dabbed on English Leather in front of the bathroom mirror Dad stood in the doorway.

"You're not going out with Bonnie are you?"

"No, Dad, I'm seeing Chrissy again."

"Good, good, she's a pretty little thing. I'm glad you're seeing her."

He stood there with his newspaper in his hand fidgeting. "Are you gonna be much longer?"

I looked at him and he stood there grinning. "Oh hell, I'm out of here," I said. He laughed as I hurried past him. He was still laughing as he closed the door to the danger zone.

I turned left off Denver Avenue onto Fifteenth Street and headed east toward Trenton Street. I sang along with the Rolling Stones doing "Satisfaction." A few minutes later Bonnie was seated next to me and we headed for the Admiral Twin Drive-in. We watched the movie for a few minutes and then started kissing. Suddenly we heard a little boy's voice yell loudly, "Hey Daddy, he's got his hand in that lady's shirt!" Bonnie screamed and lay down in the front seat. I turned and looked to my left. The five-year-old boy just stared at me. I looked past the little boy, the child's parents were smiling at me. I returned their smile then pleaded for Bonnie to sit up, but she wouldn't budge. She lay there laughing as she buttoned her blouse. Since she wouldn't sit up I decided to join her and we lay together like a couple of spoons. We talked and laughed. I nibbled on her ear and kissed her neck. I slowly opened my eyes and to my horror I saw sunlight! OH MY GOD!!! "Bonnie, wake up!" I looked at my watch, it was a little after seven o'clock. Bonnie sat up. "Oh, no, what happened?"

"Looks like we fell asleep, Bon."

"I think we've had it," she said as she wiped the sleep from her eyes. "Well, there's nothing we can do now. What's done is done."

I started the car and as we drove home I told her that this was just like the Everly Brothers song "Wake Up, Little Suzie," and she laughed. "I'll never forget this as long as I live," she said, then she kissed me. I told her that I was going to tell her parents what had happened, but she pleaded for me not to interfere. She didn't want me to walk her to the porch or even speak to her parents. When I arrived home I called her house and Mrs. Hall answered the phone. I explained everything to her. She was most cordial and admitted that she liked me a lot and that all the nonsense was caused by her overprotective husband. I apologized again for my error and hung up the phone. I knew what I had to do. I didn't like the idea of breaking up, but I couldn't put Bonnie through more hard times. On Monday morning I waited for Bonnie at her locker. I smiled as I saw her walking down the hallway toward me. She saw me, but she did not wave. Her eyes were red, and I knew that I had made the right decision. "Bonnie, don't cry," were the first words out of my mouth.

"Oh, Vincent, I hate him so much. We haven't done anything wrong. Why can't he just leave us alone?"

"Listen Bonnie, I want you to start dating."

"I don't want to date anyone else. I want you."

"It's the best thing for us. This isn't fair sneaking around like we've been doing. You don't deserve this."

"We can make it work, Vincent. A few more months and we'll be off to college, please try, honey, try?"

It would have been easy to say yes, but I knew that I had to say no. I took a deep breath and looked into her beautiful brown eyes, "It's over, Bonnie. You're free from everything."

"Just like that?" she asked, her eyes searching my face.

"There's no other way, Bon." Her eyes filled with tears. I leaned forward to kiss her and she turned her head.

"Goodbye, baby," I said softly. She looked at me as she held her books in front of her. She mouthed the word "Bye" but no sound came forth as tears streamed down her face. She turned and slowly walked away as the bell rang for classes to begin. She disappeared in the crowd, and I stood there with a huge lump in my throat. I felt my eyes start to water, and I quickly turned and walked the other away. It's the best thing for her, she won't have to suffer because of me, I said to myself. I cursed myself for being Mexican. The next month was awkward for me. I intentionally changed my route to classes so that I would not see Bonnie. "Out of sight, out of mind" was an old adage I'd heard and it seemed to work for me.

I kept busy after school visiting friends and going to football games. Central had a lousy football team, and Joey Grayson, who played for Rogers High School, was the best running back in the city. I hated his name, more out of jealousy than anything else. I'd never even talked to the guy, yet I despised him. I found out later that Lizzie Grayson, who lived next door to my Grandma McIntosh, was Joey's grandmother. Then I felt better about him somehow, at least he was Creek.

Junior was home, he had graduated from the Oklahoma School for the Deaf. He was working at a little Mexican restaurant on Eighteenth Street. Every night I would pick him up around eleven o'clock and bring him home. On this one particular night everything seemed routine. Junior got into the car and made a motion like he was wiping sweat from his brow, and I laughed at him as he lit a cigarette. We pulled out into the one-way street and drove to the stop sign a block away. As I braked, a police car with lights flashing pulled in front of me and blocked me off, then another pulled in behind me. Great, what did I do now? I stepped from the car and walked toward the police car behind me. I was wearing jeans and a long football jersey. I reached for my wallet and suddenly doors flew open on both squad cars. "Freeze!" I heard someone yell and I heard shotguns being chambered. I stopped dead in my tracks. I was ordered to the ground, slowly I assumed a spread-eagle position. Then I heard them yelling at Junior who sat in the car staring at the bizarre scene.

"Out of the car now! Out of the car or we'll shoot!" I heard the cops say over their PA system.

"He's deaf!" I yelled, "he's a deaf-mute!"

Slowly the cops emerged from behind their car doors, guns trained on me. I told them that Junior worked at the restaurant up the street and that I had just picked him up from work. They checked the car and the trunk,

Great-grandfather Temiye Kernels (*right*), holding his walking stick. The strap to his medicine pouch can be seen across his chest. The photo was taken in Holdenville, Indian Territory.

FILIACION

Señas particulares ... Una cicatr

en la ceja izquierda.

Estatura ... 5' 6"

Color ... moreno

Ojos ... negros

Barba ... no usa.

Edad ... 3? años.

Profesión ... minero

Residencia ... Tulsa,Okla.

Blas Mendoza
Firma del interesado

Estado Civil ... casado

Left. Blas Mendoza, 1929

Below left. Great-grand-parents Alex and Martha McIntosh with their children. Newman McIntosh, my grandfather, is in the back row at right.

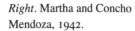

Right. Martha and Concho Mendoza, 1942.

Below. *(left to right)* Junior, Dad, and Linda. I am in the foreground.

Left. Mom (*left*) and Grandma McIntosh.

Above. Claude Mendoza and His Mariachis. Standing, (*left to right*) Charlie, Ray, Victor, Claude, and Concho Mendoza; foreground, Vince Mendoza.

Charlie (*left*) and Concho Mendoza.

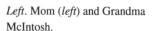

Above Left. Linda Mendoza Dellinger.

Above. Deborah Chelf Mendoza.

Left. Vincent Mendoza, Phu Bai, 1968.

Above. Vincent and Debbie Mendoza at Six Flags, June 1970.

Above right. Felicia Ann Mendoza (*left*) and Micaela Mendoza.

Below. Micaela Mendoza at eighteen.

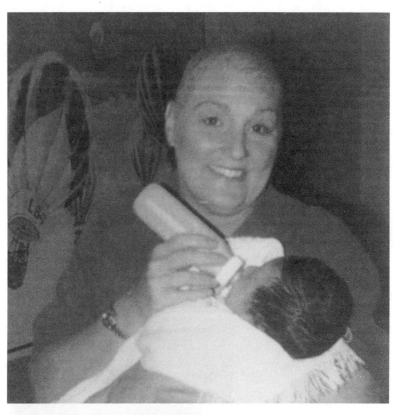

Above. Debbie and Terri.

Left. Lance Anthony DeGraw.

Right. Felicia and Terri.

Vincent Mendoza, 1994.

then apologized. They had been looking for two armed robbers who were driving the same make car as mine. They let us go and I signed to Junior and told him they were after two robbers. He motioned to me and himself, then he laughed. Junior and I got along great, but I felt sorry for him because Mom and Dad were overprotective. I guess since he was handicapped they assumed that he couldn't make it in the real world. Maybe he could, maybe he couldn't, but they never gave him the chance. He was by no means stupid, he was sharp, and we enjoyed each other's company. On another occasion I was waiting in the small parking lot for Junior to get off work when Pepe Garza, a waiter, came running out the back door. He ran to my car, "Vicente, I got two girls coming around back. Keep one busy while I take the other one to José's car. You're my brother, and you don't speak English, okay?"

"Sure, Pepe, sure."

He smiled and took a roll of breath mints out of his pocket and put one in his mouth. Just then two girls came around the corner. They were both cute, and one of them ran to Pepe and kissed him full on the mouth. They walked to the darkened alleyway while the other girl stood by my car. She looked at me and smiled. "Hi," she said.

"No speak de Inglesa."

"My name's Sharon, I go to T.U."

I smiled and nodded my head, then she began talking to herself. She didn't know why she was talking to me at all since I couldn't speak English. "You, Pepe's brother?"

"Sí, Pepe," I said as I stepped from the car.

She looked around and shuffled her feet, then she looked at me and smiled, "Four score and seven years ago our fathers brought forth on this continent," then she giggled as I looked at her and smiled. She reached into her purse and pulled out a pack of cigarettes and lit one. She blew the smoke into the night air. She looked me up and down, then giggled again, "You know you're cute," she said smiling broadly. "You Mexican boys are hot, real hot, did you know that?"

"No speak de Inglesa."

She laughed out loud, and I was dying, "I bet you can really do it, huh, baby?" I took the cigarette from her and took a drag, then coughed. She put her hand on my shoulder. "Oh, what I could teach you amigo," she said, looking into my eyes. I put my hands on her waist. "Oooh!" she cooed. I wanted to talk to her, but I knew she was quite a bit older than I was, probably a senior at the University of Tulsa, and there was no way she would date me, this was just fun for both of us. I pulled her close and smiled. "Sí, sí," she said. My heart rate quickened and just as I was about to kiss her Pepe and the other girl came out from the alley. Sharon jumped back and straightened her clothes. The other girl laughed at her, "Sharon, what have you been doing with Pepe's little brother? You ought to be ashamed." Then the two girls said goodbye and disappeared around the corner. Pepe thanked me and we laughed about the cute gringas. A few minutes later Junior came out and we drove home.

Saturday morning we drove to Okmulgee, Mom and Dad in the front seat, Junior and I in the back. It wasn't the long trip it had been years before. The "Beeline" had been completed and we took the four-lane highway nonstop to Okmulgee. It was quiet at the camp house, none of the hustle and bustle that had been evident when Grandpa was alive, there were fewer visitors and guests. Grandma was content. She had her children and her grandchildren to look after, and that seemed to keep her busy. She still laughed and talked like she always had. Aunt Lucy lived in Okmulgee so Grandma never got lonely. She took care of Brenda, Charley, Tommy, and little Danny. Like a true grandma she loved all her grandchildren. She had a hug for any of us and was happy as she scolded us with mock anger.

The cold February wind blew as I answered the knock at the door. Wayne stood on my front porch in his winter greens, a single red chevron on each sleeve and an "expert rifleman" badge on his chest along with a single ribbon. "Don't ever in your life join the Marine Corps" were his first words and I laughed as I invited him into our house. Wayne had only twenty days of leave, then he would have to report back to Camp Pendleton, California. Once there he would be sent to his permanent assignment. He spent most of his time with Leslie, but we managed a few pool games and some poker with the guys, then all too soon he was gone. At that time in my life I never thought of death. Death only happened to old people. Wayne would be fine. He would serve his country, come home, marry Leslie, and live happily ever after. Life was cool.

On April Fool's Day as I walked toward "The Great Spirit" I had to smile when the bronze statue came into view. Draped across one open palm the Indian chief had a bra, in the other hand was a pair of panties. Students walked by giggling, evidently a teacher had yet to spy the added garments. I continued the walk to my locker. Suddenly I saw her and I felt nauseated. It was Bonnie, and she was walking with a geek! Oh my God! She smiled when she saw me, our eyes met, she passed without saying a word. I turned to look at the guy she was walking with. Oh Bonnie, you can do better than that, I thought. I had seen the guy before, he was the king of geeks. He wore a tie to school for Christ's sake. He carried a brief-case and in his shirt pocket were no less than thirty-six pens and pencils. Not only that, but he wore white socks with dark pants. Oh Bonnie, what have I done? I stood there as they disappeared in the crowd. I shrugged my shoulders, well, as long as she's happy that's all that matters, then I looked down at my own attire. Penny loafers, wheat jeans, and a madras shirt. Me, a geek? Naw . . . no way.

It was late May, I had just come home from school when the phone rang. It was Donnie Hamilton, Wayne's little brother, and he was crying. He didn't have to say anything. I knew. The official report read that Lance Corporal Floyd Wayne Hamilton had been killed while defending his po-sition. That night I cried. The thought of my friend dying was unbeliev-able. He was so young, he had so much to live for, and now he was gone forever. A million thoughts crossed my mind. He would never see his family again or enjoy fatherhood. I tried to grasp the reality that my buddy was dead, I couldn't believe he was gone. This can't be happening I thought, maybe I'll wake up and this will all be a horrible dream, but it was no dream. That night on the local news the main story was "Another Tulsan Killed in South Vietnam." I grew sullen and distant. The funeral was on a Thursday at one o'clock. I left school at noon and hurried home to change into my only suit. It was dark blue and real baggy. I drove to the funeral home. I felt numb as I entered the chapel. I signed the register and sat in the back alone. Soon the service was over and it was time to view the body. As I walked up to the casket I was transfixed. Wayne was in his dress blues, his body in a full-length glass case, and his skin looked oily. Oh God, why did you do this to him? I turned and slowly walked to my car. The drive to the graveyard seemed to take forever. As I got out of my car the Marine Corps Honor Guard was removing the gray casket from the black hearse. The air was hot, the slight breeze felt like a furnace blowing in my face. The old reverend found himself fighting back tears as he stood near Wayne's casket, and as he ended his prayer the Honor Guard fired a twenty-one-gun salute. Somewhere in the distance a lone trumpet could be heard playing "Taps." I had heard "Taps" several times on television, but until you've actually lost someone close to you, you don't realize how this song tears at your heart. I thought of Wayne and Leslie. I watched Wayne's mother and Leslie hold each other and cry.

Suddenly my chin began to tremble and tears rushed from my eyes. I stood away from the crowd. I felt a hand on my right shoulder and slowly turned around to see who was trying to comfort me. No one was there. I looked all around me. No one had been close enough to touch me. I knew that it must be Wayne. I wasn't afraid. Being Indian I believed in the invisible world. I accepted the fact that my friend was near. It was then I swore revenge for my friend. "They'll pay, Wayne, they'll pay," I muttered. I walked over to Wayne's family. We were all still in shock. I knelt down as Leslie reached out for my hand. We held each other and cried. I never told anyone of my plans to enlist, or the reason why. College could wait.

SEVEN // **Special Delivery Marine**

With graduation behind me I was ready to enlist in the Marines. In June 1966 Harry Nunnally, a friend of mine from Central High, and I entered the recruiter's office together. Boy, was that recruiter ever friendly. I believe he would have lent us money had we asked. "What can I do for you men?" inquired the beaming sergeant.

"We're ready to sign up," I said, and the recruiter rubbed his hands together. Harry and I looked at each other. The hand rubbing was a bad sign.

"What do you want to do in the Marines?" asked Smiley.

"Give me infantry or artillery," was my reply.

"You got it, son. Sign on the dotted line."

We would not leave for a few weeks, so the month of June I partied.

It was mid-June and Mom, Dad, Junior, and I stopped at Linda and Ron's house to pick up Linda and the kids for a picnic. Ron had to work that weekend. Soon we were on the shores of Keystone Lake. We fished and played in the water. We had grand fun and then all too soon it was time to leave. I sat in the backseat of our '65 Pontiac Catalina as it sped down the highway toward Tulsa. I held four-month-old Kevin in his baby carrier. I looked at him and he smiled at me. I thought to myself, sorry I have to leave you, little fella, but there's something I have to do. I'll come back to you, and by that time you'll be old enough to remember me, how's that? He kicked his little legs and waved his hands, and I smiled at him. I hated leaving Dina and Kevin. I wanted to be there for them. I'd make it up to them when I returned and that was a promise.

With all the goodbyes said, Harry and I were on our way to the Marine Corps Recruit Depot in San Diego, California. There were ten of us from Oklahoma that had either joined or been drafted into the Marine Corps. Seated next to me on the commercial jet was another Indian boy, Sam Beaver. He was dark-skinned and he talked so slow that at times I wanted to grab him by the collar and yell at him to hurry up. "How long did you sign up for?" I asked.

"Four years," he said, "and Mama's sure gonna be mad."

"Why?"

"Well, I came down here to Oklahoma City to see my friend off. He joined the Navy. Anyway, this fella got to talking to me and the next thing I know I'm on this here jet headed for the Marine Corps. I was supposed to milk the cows when I got home tonight. Mama's gonna kill me."

At ten o'clock that evening we landed in San Diego. A real nice sergeant, greeted us warmly in the airport terminal, but as soon as we boarded the gray Navy bus he suddenly changed into a snarling, foulmouthed, ranting mad dog. The verbal abuse continued throughout the night, and I thought of Dad and smiled to myself. Dad was rather drab compared to this guy, but hey, this guy was a pro. They shaved our heads and we were issued our first military clothing. Somewhere during the night we showered, and finally around three in the morning we were allowed to sleep for two hours. Days passed, it was exhausting. We were issued more gear and we started learning how to march. The drill instructor (DI) bid us goodnight, "Goodnight you little fuckers, I'll see your asses in the morning!" When the lights were turned off I couldn't believe my ears, I could hear guys crying. We heard explosions too . . . it was the Fourth of July, 1966.

Boot camp was usually eight weeks, but we had to wait two extra weeks for our series to form. The verbal abuse continued at an accelerated pace as well as the physical punishment. It was like a fraternity hazing; if you wanted to be a part of the club you had to pass the test just like everyone else.

While we were at the rifle range I had an experience I will never forget. During May 1966 I'd had a dream that I was in a small airplane with "Champagne" Tony Lema, a professional golfer. I was behind him and the pilot in the aircraft. I was not a person, I was an observer. The pilot spoke to Tony Lema.

"We've got trouble Tony, I gotta set her down."

"There's a golf course up ahead, let's set her down on a fairway."

"Sounds good, let's give it a try," the pilot replied.

Suddenly I was no longer in the plane, I was on the golf course. I watched in horror as the aircraft slammed into the ground and erupted in a ball of fire. I woke up sweating and breathing hard. I shrugged it off as a nightmare and thought nothing else of it until I opened the Sunday paper that day at the rifle range. The headlines read, "Tony Lema Dies in Plane Crash on Golf Course"! I almost died myself. During my teen years I had experienced déjà vu on a few occasions, but this was the first time I had ever had a precognitive dream. It was not to be the last.

Graduation drew closer and we were in the best physical shape of our young lives; even those who had suffered the worst mental stress were now tough individuals. Physically and mentally we were prepared for whatever lay ahead. I had qualified for Sea School, which meant that if chosen I would be assigned to Marine Liaison on board a ship. Twenty of us from different platoons stood at ease as a sergeant walked up and down eyeballing each one. He picked three individuals and the rest of us were sent back to our platoons. Our DI also asked if any of us could play a musical instrument and I kept my mouth shut. I didn't want to spend four years polishing a saxophone. The day before graduation Sergeant Ramirez called us into one of the Quonset huts.

"I'm going to read off your MOS, your Military Occupational Specialty," he yelled and everyone talked at once. As he called the first name the room was silent.

"Private Allen . . . Camp Pendleton, Motor T."

"What's that?" we all asked.

"You're a truck driver!" smiled Ramirez.

"Damn," came the reply and we all laughed.

"Private Baca . . . Camp Pendleton, Headquarters Company, Supply.

"Private Collins . . . Infantry. Congratulations, Private, you're a grunt."

Everyone cheered, everyone except Collins, who had been drafted. He hung his head and looked down. Finally it was my turn, and I eagerly awaited my MOS.

"Private Mendoza . . . Camp Pendleton, Headquarters Company, Postal."

"Sir, what is Postal, sir?"

"You're a fucking mailman!" Everyone hooted and hollered as I stood with my mouth open. I couldn't believe it. I'd signed up for infantry and I end up a mailman? The next day we graduated full of pride and honor, glad that we didn't have to endure any more. We marched back to our huts, gathered our gear, and separately headed for our respective buses. We would not go to war as one unit, we were each on our own.

I came home on leave toward the end of October. It's funny how things seem to change after you've been away. You don't know if it's you that's changed or everything else. After high school graduation everyone had scattered. No one was home. They were in college or working. It was a strange feeling. There were thousands of people in Tulsa and yet it was a ghost town to me. I was home, but it was not the same . . . it would never be the same.

When I returned to Camp Pendleton in November I was ready for anything. Rested and eager, I approached the white two-story barracks located in the 24 area of Camp Pendleton. No one was around as I walked into the squad bay. I found an empty lower bunk and unpacked my gear. Thirty minutes later the squad bay began to fill with young Marines from the day shift. I met a kid from Arkansas, Jeff Trumaine. We went to chow together and then returned to the barracks. It was dark now, except for the building's two porch lights.

I heard someone yell, "Field day!" and my heart sank. I hated "field days." The thought of cleaning toilets and mopping floors on my first day back was not in my plans. I looked around as privates and PFCs scurried inside the barracks. No one was watching as I slipped over the rail of the porch. I hit the ground and crawled under the porch, into the darkness. I had just relaxed and was feeling quite proud of myself for dodging the work detail when suddenly a Zippo lighter flared in front of my face. I let out a little yelp as a chunky, curly-haired Marine lit his cigarette.

"What took you so long?" he asked. Then he laughed and stuck out his hand. "Charlie Laker, Detroit, Michigan." Soon another Marine joined us, Larry Price from La Mesa, California. Larry was short with brown hair and a sprinkle of freckles. We would become the best of friends. After the field day was over we walked into the barracks and Charlie introduced me to Santos, a young Chicano. He had dark eyes and jet black hair combed straight back. He was well muscled with a narrow waist. We exchanged greetings and then walked back with Santos to the card game that Laker had interrupted.

"Where are you from?" a fellow called J. C. asked.

"Oklahoma," I replied.

"Bonus Nachos," quipped a big blond kid named Schaeller.

"Bonus," I replied, and the big kid grinned broadly. He was tall, his flattop haircut was too long but still stood straight up, giving him the appearance of being scared all the time. His voice sounded like the actor Lee Marvin's.

"Pleased to meet you," Plummer said as he stuck out his hand. Plummer was a square-jawed fellow with a five o'clock shadow. He was the only Marine in the barracks that actually needed to shave in the evening. We all talked, while Plummer was raking in the money at the makeshift poker table.

The next morning came early. By five-thirty we were all standing in formation in front of the barracks. A young black sergeant stepped to the front of the formation. He wore a starched Marine Corps–issue cover (cap) and green fatigues. Broad-shouldered and narrow-waisted, he looked to be in shape. He led us in calisthenics and then announced that we were going on a two-mile run. I whispered to Laker, "Ever see John Wayne run?"

Laker raised his index finger and with a matter-of-fact look said, "Once."

We ran through the 24 area, which was our headquarters area. It was also home to every single female Marine on base. I felt like a fox in a chickenhouse. As we jogged in step through the early morning darkness, the only sound you could hear was the pounding of our boots on the black-topped streets.

I was assigned to a small post office with Sergeant Braig. We drove there in his car. He was a wormy little guy. He wore thick glasses and his hair was slicked down. You could tell he was married because he had this bored look about him. There was no pep in his step, no pizazz. He was just there, and heaven forbid, somebody had married this guy? . . . get real. Anyway, he was my mentor.

The job was a piece of cake. I sold stamps, mailed packages, and sorted mail for the units in my area. The charts were simple enough to follow when it came to weighing packages and sending them to various locations in the States. I also learned the difference between certified and registered mail. Sergeant Braig was quick to let me know that any tampering or mishandling of the mail was a federal charge. They could make room in the brig for anyone who thought he could beat the system. I also sold money orders to the troops. I felt good about being in the post office. I was the link between these lonesome kids and home. I shouldn't really say kids, although most of them were. I should say Marines, because men of all ages and ranks stood before me, baby-faced PFCs, old gunnery sergeants, young and old officers alike. I was the link to loved ones back home. Money orders were sent to wives or parents and, even more valuable, photos to and from home. Photos that brought loved ones close again. Photos of a newborn baby sent to a father who might never hold his child, or see his child except for the photos we delivered. No, this was not a job. This was an obligation. We were the messengers of hope. We provided dreams. We delivered Christmas every day of the year, and when in combat we delivered the will to live, to conquer, to survive. Letters from home, pure gold from the heart.

It was five o'clock on a Friday when Laker, Price, and I showered and got ready to go in to Oceanside. As we stepped off the bus I was surprised to see nothing but young Marines. I had girls on my mind, but as far as I could see there was nothing but shaved heads. We walked up and down the main street of Oceanside checking out the many pawn shops and photography studios.

"Hey look, it's Trumaine," Laker said as he pointed to a tattoo shop across the street. We hurried over and sure enough, there was Jeff Trumaine sitting in the front window getting a tattoo on his arm.

"Whatcha got there, hillbilly?" Laker asked as we walked into the shop. "Is it a cobra or a skull-and-crossbones?"

"Shucks no. I got me a bulldog with a helmet cocked on the side of his head."

The tattooer turned and smiled. "Who's next?" he asked. His black hair was curly and greasy, he had a cigarette hanging from the side of his mouth. He had that look of a wolf when he sees a flock of sheep.

"Not me," I said.

"I'm next," Price said, stepping forward. The tattooer smiled and went back to work on Trumaine's arm. Laker and I laughed as Larry browsed through the many patterns of tattoos.

"Hey, Larry, Laker and I will meet you and Jeff over at the USO in about an hour," I said. As we headed out the door, I turned and saw Price eyeballing this huge cobra with a bayonet between its teeth (pirate style). I told Charlie and we both laughed as we walked down the street. We entered a little Mexican restaurant and spied Robert Santos and Donnie Schaeller sitting at a table. They looked at us and smiled.

"Ola, muchachos," Schaeller said, then he turned in his chair and spoke to the waitress. "Cuatro cervezas, por favor."

Santos slapped the blue-eyed blond on the back and laughed.

"Listen to him speak that Spanish."

"Yep, my Pappy done had me speaking Spanish when I quit nursing, besides there's a lot of pretty Mexican girls in Phoenix." Then he grinned real big, making sure to show all his teeth. Laker had his very first plate of Mexican food and raved about it so much that the flattered señoras didn't even charge him for the meal. Later we went down to the USO and shot some pool and enjoyed a dance with some chaperoned girls. Punch and cookies were served free of charge.

On 1 December 1966 a quota came in for Westpac (Western Pacific Duty). Laker, Knapp, Mendoza, Santos, Schaeller, Price, Plummer, Roland, and Perry were the names on the list. We were sent to staging battalion. We were on our way overseas. Staging battalion was a month-long school in which all phases of combat were reviewed. We were called to formation one day and to our surprise our commanding officer (CO) granted us five days of leave. I arrived in Tulsa flat broke, all my money spent on airfare home. I noticed a police officer on duty at the airport terminal and I walked up to him in my winter greens and asked if I could borrow a dime for a phone call. He told me to get lost . . . what a jerk. Finally a nice girl from one of the rental car agencies let me use her phone, and thirty minutes later Mom and Dad picked me up at the airport. It started snowing as we drove home. Four days passed quickly, and as I hugged my family at the terminal gate I wondered if I would ever see them again. I remembered Wayne not coming back. I acted cheerful as I said my goodbyes, I didn't want to upset Mama any more than she already was. From my window seat in the American Airlines 727 I waved my handkerchief as Mama had requested, and they waved back at the white cloth. I felt a large lump in my throat, thinking maybe this was the last goodbye, then I shrugged the feeling off. Hey, I'm a United States Marine, knock it off, quit feeling wimpy. I cleared my throat and erased my sentimental thoughts. As the plane lifted off the ground my mind was already in California.

It was 11 January 1967 when we headed south down the coast. All was quiet on the bus, each boy alone with his thoughts, each thinking the same thing . . . will I return? When we arrived in San Diego we stepped down from the bus and filed in a line to board the ship. It was just like one of the many movies that I had watched a million times on the late show, only this time I was in it. We looked sharp in our green fatigues, each of us wearing a camouflaged helmet and battle pack, cartridge belts fastened at the waist, bayonets hanging off the belt and tied to one leg. We each carried a green seabag. As we got closer to the ship I could hear a band playing "Stars and Stripes Forever." A crowd was beginning to gather as fifteen hundred Marines and a thousand army personnel eased toward the ship. The ship was the U.S.S. *Walker*, a retired merchant vessel that had been taken out of dry dock somewhere up the coast. I heard my name called and I answered with a "Yo" and headed up the gangplank. Hours later the ship began to move, and ever so slowly we pulled away from the dock and headed out to sea. As we left the harbor we were followed by fifty or so boats. Some were fancy cruisers, others were fishing boats. They all blew their horns or rang their bells and the people aboard waved to us. One by one the boats dropped back and soon the skyline disappeared. We were on our way. It was evening now and the sea was calm.

J. C. Knapp and I stood watching the gulls sail above the ship. He was from Los Angeles. He was fair-skinned, his mother was Mexican and his father white. He was likable and quiet. I attributed that to his age, he was an old-timer, twenty-three years old. We hadn't been under way more than fifteen minutes when the first Marine bent over the rail and lost his lunch. Then another and another, until the entire rail was covered with bodies leaning over the side. One of the merchant seamen walked by me, looked at that line-up, and shook his head. "Tell ya what," he said, "look at the horizon and not the water, and always keep something in your stomach, and you won't wind up like the rest of those guys." I never forgot what he said. Down below it was worse. We were packed like sardines. Vomit sloshed around freely, and every morning a crew of men would hose the compartments down.

One day when I ventured to the rear of the boat to use the rest room, the sea was getting rough. The toilets had no stalls. Fifteen bare toilet seats to a row, and there were four rows. Around the toilets were little handrails. I sat down a seat away from five other Marines who sat there facing each other and talking as if they were on a park bench. One of them asked another about the handrails, and just at that moment we found ourselves five feet in the air with our pants around our ankles. The ship had dropped in the rough seas, leaving us airborne for an instant. As we started back down, the ship came up, and we slammed into the floor with our pants still around our ankles. Making my way out of the head I heard one of the other Marines say, "You just had to ask, didn't ya?"

We ran out of fresh water for showering four days out to sea. There's nothing quite like a saltwater shower. The soap doesn't lather, and you feel sticky all over. I never showered again on that journey. The food was terrible also. Scuttlebutt was the officers were eating high on the hog, while we were served toast, coffee, apples, powdered eggs, powdered milk, and powdered powder. I survived on apples, toast, and coffee for twenty-one days.

We were called to formation one day and a captain asked for volunteers for a secret mission. Laker stood behind me, he eased forward and whispered in my ear, "I wonder if he's going to volunteer." I smiled as I thought, no way José. Someone behind us asked how many volunteers were needed and the captain replied, "Five hundred men." Laker leaned forward again and whispered in my ear, "Yeah, and I'd like to kiss a fat lady's ass, too!" I smiled again. The next day we were informed that not enough men had volunteered and we listened as the captain called the names of the unlucky souls who had been chosen to fill the complement. Suddenly I heard my name, Mendoza, V. L., as well as Santos, R. E., Knapp J. C., Perry, B. G. We, the chosen, were moved to the front of the ship. Our heads were shaved, and we were told to write one letter only and not mention our mission. The letter would be censored before the envelope was sealed. We sat on the deck at the front of the ship, and Donnie Schaeller came sneaking around the corner. "Howdy, boys! Well, well, ya know," he paused for a moment, "y'all look like a bunch of buzzards," and then he grinned real big, showing all his teeth.

"Real funny, Shael, real funny, man," J. C. said.

Schaeller spoke again. "I noticed they got all the Mexicans on board for this here secret mission. You don't reckon they're going back after the Alamo, do ya?" Then he showed all his teeth again.

"That's right man, they did pick all the Mexicans," Santos said with a stern look. Then his face lit up and he began to laugh. "They even got J. C. and he looks like a white boy." We all laughed and J. C. got mad and jumped up. "I can't get killed, I only signed up for two years!"

Then Schaeller spoke again, "My pappy always said . . . "

"Oh, go fuck your pappy!" J. C. yelled and stormed off.

"I don't think Pappy would like that," Schaeller replied, looking at us and grinning.

The next day we docked on the island of Okinawa. We were assigned to the Ninth Marine Amphibious Brigade. As I walked down the gangplank I yelled goodbye to my friends who would continue on to Vietnam.

"Hey, Price, don't catch anything!"

"Hey, Vince, I'm telling Pappy that you chickened out!" Schaeller yelled.

"Hey, Laker, I'll drink a cold one for ya!" I yelled.

"Asshole!" Laker laughed, as he waved his middle finger at me.

Sure hope they make it, I thought, I really do. Then we were herded onto buses and headed for Camp Hansen, home of the brigade. We were there two days before we got the good news . . . the secret mission had been scrapped. One week later we were granted liberty and I became a man, thanks to one of the "ladies of the night" in the village we called Kin Ville. We were assigned to the Ninth Marine Amphibious Brigade Post Office and for the next thirteen months we partied hearty. Somewhere along the way I was promoted to lance corporal. To my surprise Bonnie started writing me. She was still going with the geek and they were together at Oklahoma State University. I felt pretty stupid for giving her up, but I just couldn't stand seeing her cry.

A couple of months into my stay on "Okie" we found out about our secret mission. My friends and I would have been among the first Marines to land on the shores of North Vietnam. I felt as if I had a spirit watching over me. Was it Little Grandma, or my Waleeta, or maybe even Wayne? The thirteen months seemed to fly by, and to my chagrin I spoke Japanese better than I did Spanish or Creek. I served with some great guys on Okinawa. The memories I have of those days would last a lifetime.

One favorite memory is my departure from Okinawa. We were all milling around waiting to board a commercial airliner when I noticed an old gunnery sergeant moving real slow. I figured he had been wounded in Nam. Although the day was bright and sunny he wore his military issue raincoat. We boarded the airliner and to our displeasure the stewardess informed us that they would not be serving any liquor on the fourteen-hour flight. The plane began to move, and when it lifted off the ground a loud cheer rang throughout the cabin. As we circled the island I looked down at the view below. So long Kin Ville, adios Moon Beach and Kadena. I'm going home. For some reason I started thinking about an old country western song, "Way down yonder in the Indian nation, rode my pony on the reservation in those Oklahoma hills where I was born." Twenty-five minutes later the old gunnery sergeant walked to the front of the plane. All eyes were on him as he turned to face us, opened his raincoat flasher style, and let everyone see the six bottles of whiskey that he had sewn into the lining. Another cheer rocked the plane.

As I stepped off the plane in Tulsa I saw Mama, smiling along with Dad and Junior. She ran to me and hugged me as Dad and Junior patted me on the back. We left the airport arm in arm. It was good to be home. I soon knew what royalty felt like. I was waited on hand and foot, I couldn't get anything for myself. Mom would bring plate after plate of food, and as soon as Dad got in from work he was beside me telling me about his work and the problems he was having with his golf game. I was getting back in the groove of talking sign language with Junior. Being home felt good, but I felt smothered at times.

I visited friends and relatives. A week before I was to leave I went to see Uncle Claude. He had been ill with liver problems. I had been to one of the Mexican dances where Dad and the rest of the family played, but Claude was ill at home. I missed his hearty laughter, but most of all I missed his singing and fiddle playing. We visited all day. I enjoyed the time we shared. All too soon it was time to leave. I shook his hand, his once strong handshake was gone. I had a feeling that I would never see him again. I looked into his tired eyes and hugged him. His eyes watered, "You be careful, Banson, take care of yourself. Don't let them hurt you." He slapped my back as we hugged.

"I'll be careful, Tío." Claude died eight days later.

A few days after that, Arnold called and invited me to a fraternity party at Northeastern State. The next afternoon I drove to Tahlequah. It was a mild day for March and I dressed casual with a light jacket. I walked around the campus. I was in no hurry. I just wanted to walk around and imagine myself as a freshman. I watched couples strolling hand in hand, while others scurried by, probably late for class. I felt awkward and out of place. I thought how great it would be to go to school here. To be on the football team and enjoy the company of a nice girl instead of bar whores. The campus was quiet and serene. What a change from Okinawa. Kin Ville was filled with young men going to or coming from war. They didn't give a damn. If they were going to war they raised hell; after all what did they have to lose, they might not come back at all. And if they were returning they were so happy and carefree, almost crazy, they had made it through hell. I sat on a bench and savored the peace and quiet. I looked at my watch, it was time to find Scholars' Bar. As I stood up I looked around the campus one last time, then I smiled. Coming toward me was a geek. Highwater pants, briefcase, and a pocketful of pens. As he passed, I turned and watched him walk out of sight. He's in his own little world, I thought, then I realized that I was too. I shook my head and headed for Scholars' Bar.

Twenty-four hours later I was checking into Headquarters Company in the 24 area of Camp Pendleton. I entered the squad bay and found an empty rack (bunk). After unpacking I lay down to catch some sleep. I dozed and thought of the pretty coed that I had met at Scholars' Bar. As I slept I could hear a voice. It sounded like Lee Marvin singing "El Paso." I smiled, there was only one guy in the whole world who could sound that awful, and he sang "El Paso" at least once a day all the way across the Pacific . . . Schaeller. I opened one eye and there he stood singing his heart out at the foot of my rack. He stopped and looked at me. "Cómo está frijoles?" he asked. That was his Spanish for "How have you bean?" It was good to see Don again and soon everyone that I had origi- nally shipped out with returned to the squad bay, all except Plummer. He had been killed near Chu Lai while making a mail run to an outpost. That night we all sat around talking about Nam and Okie. It was good to be with my friends again.

I worked the evening shift at Camp Pendleton. As I entered the direc- tory section everyone was busy. They passed without speaking, answer- ing phones, sacking mail. There were a few women Marines, but mostly civilian ladies worked the large directory books on day shift. The directo- ries had the name of every Marine that had been stationed at Camp Pen- dleton within the past thirty days. The large books were alphabetized and were updated daily. Each book was accompanied by a phone. They were placed on long tables that formed a horseshoe around the large room. The information they contained was names, serial numbers, companies, and information letting us know if each individual was still on base or had been shipped overseas or to another base in the United States.

By summer I had fallen in love with Cindy, a woman Marine. She was blonde-haired and blue-eyed, older than I was but we were too crazy about each other to worry about two little years. She was intelligent, sassy, and beautiful. She was the best thing that ever happened to me. She wanted to marry, but I didn't feel right about being married while I was in the Corps. She was discharged and agreed to wait for me. I had finally found someone to come back to. A reason to survive. Cindy was my dream come true. A month after her discharge Price and I volunteered for Nam. At staging battalion Larry and I were separated. He went to the Air Wing company, and lucky me, I got the First Marine Division. Another month passed and I was on my way.

EIGHT // **The Warrior Within**

The old gunnery sergeant's voice boomed into the squad bay, "First platoon, saddle up!" We boarded the Navy bus that would take us to El Toro, a Marine air station. There was no laughter, each of us alone with our thoughts. I looked at the mixture of men. Chicanos, Indians, blacks, whites, Orientals, we were all there. I savored everything I looked at. Look at that GTO, a flock of pigeons, a bread truck, stupid things that didn't mean squat took on new meaning when you stopped to think you might not ever see them again. I gazed at the surf and thought of Cindy, the times we'd talked, played, and made love on the beaches of California. Families in station wagons passed our bus, the children inside waving to us and smiling, while Mom and Dad checked a road map. People were going to work, plumbers, salesmen, executives, construction workers, everything was normal except we were headed for Vietnam.

The last six hours of our flight were quiet. Vietnam was out there waiting for us. For some of us this would be our last plane ride ever. Although there were one hundred eighty of us, the cabin was silent. Suddenly, the captain's voice came over the intercom, "Please fasten your seat belts. We are beginning our descent into the Republic of South Vietnam." I had that feeling you have when you get on a roller coaster. You take the long, slow ride up and then as you near the big drop you think, here I go, I can't turn back even if I wanted to. Then you see the cars dropping off one by one in front of you, and you know that it's going to happen to you. That's exactly how I felt when the jet touched down on the runway.

As we were deplaning I looked at the young stewardess. She was pleasant-looking, with just a touch of makeup, like the typical girl next door. I wanted to hold her, cling to her, just for a moment, but then I remembered that big bad Marines are never afraid. I looked away and stepped from the plane.

The next morning four of us boarded a large truck that would take us to

First Marine Division headquarters. It was a bright clear day. The surrounding hills reminded me of the Ozarks around Eureka Springs, Arkansas, the way the roads were cut into the hillsides. We pulled out of the secured area of Da Nang and I saw my first Vietnamese, jeez they were little. We passed through a little village called "Dogpatch." It was nothing but cardboard, plywood, and tin huts. The place was filthy. Dogpatch would be a dump back home. Little street urchins stood around. One little guy in red shorts saw me looking at him as we drove past. He gave me the finger, nice place. Mama-sans squatted under shade trees chewing betel nuts, talking and laughing. They didn't care that their teeth were being blackened by the juice of the nut. Old men and young women labored under various burdens. Some carried vegetables loaded on yokes across their shoulders, others carried water. Their black pajamas were filthy and worn. The broad straw hats they wore made them look picturesque against the backdrop of palm trees. It was if I had been taken back in time. There were no luxuries here, no 7-Eleven or McDonalds to run to. No electricity or plumbing, just survival. The next day I was sent north to Phu Bai. I grabbed my gear and stepped from the C-130. I walked toward the air terminal and spotted the mail truck parked in front. "Can I get a lift to the divvy PO?" I asked.

"Are you the new guy?"

"Yep."

"Get in. Dan Sheridan, Dallas, Texas. Two hundred twenty days!" Everyone added the number of days they had left in Vietnam as if it were a part of their name or serial number. It was the most important number in the world.

Dan was a strange-looking kid. Grubby, with bushy eyebrows. He sported a mohawk haircut. His teeth were yellow from smoking and across his chest he holstered a .45 automatic pistol.

"Tell ya what, Vince, don't trust any dink, kids, women, no one. They'll blow ya away first chance they get. Roll out of your rack when the rockets and mortars come in, there's less chance of catching shrapnel that's flying around. When you get some ass take a buddy with you and stay together. Grass is going for fifty cents a bag already rolled and in plastic bags. Any kid will sell them to ya. If you see a red flare at night, you got gooks coming through the wire. You'd better find a hole and jump in."

I had a lot to learn. I listened hard to what this guy said. I didn't think about the grass he mentioned. Marijuana or any other drug had never interested me. I couldn't do that to my body, or my father's name or my mother's heart. No, Vince Mendoza would not destroy himself. I had the blood of warriors and "La Raza" in me, I would not dishonor my heritage. Only weak men needed drugs . . . I was not weak.

A black corporal showed me to our "hootch." He was a short-timer, soon he'd be back in Philadelphia. We walked across the barren compound, our boots kicking up red dust. Ahead danced four little devil dusters, twirling red dirt like mini-tornadoes. Our hootch was two hundred yards from the post office. "There's an empty rack," Nelson said, pointing to the left of the doorway. "You can use that trunk there, too," he added.

"Hey, thanks, man." I threw my forty-pound seabag and thirty-pound flak jacket down in a heap. Nelson left and I began unpacking. I sat down on my cot and loaded the empty magazines with the ammo that Nelson had given me. When I finished I lit a cigarette and looked around at my surroundings. The plywood walls came up only two feet from the floor, from there up it was all screen, all the way to the roof. The roof was tin. There was a screen door at each end of the hootch, which was forty feet long and about fifteen feet wide, with two light bulbs hanging down from the open rafters. My cot was next to the door, I liked that. Photos of family and girlfriends stood on the small trunks next to each cot. One lone card table sat in the middle of the large, open room. There were eight cots, two were unoccupied. At night a few guys would play cards. Some wrote letters home. Everyone marked off another day on his calendar.

Two weeks passed. I was on the midnight shift at Phu Bai. The nights cooled down to 115 degrees, while the day shift endured 125-degree heat. One morning after breakfast I stripped down and stretched out on my cot. I heard the screen door open and the thud of a seabag. I raised up on one elbow and looked at the doorway. Standing there was that man from the Air Wing, Larry Price. I began to laugh, Larry began to cuss. "That no good, dirty, rotten motherfucker, anyway!"

"What happened to the cold beer in Da Nang, the PXs, and hot food? You know, the good life?" I asked.

"Aw, that sneaky little fuckin' corporal on Okinawa changed my orders!"

I was really laughing now, and Price was kicking the shit out of his seabag!

A week later I was switched over to the day shift and continued to throw mail. Each unit had its own pallet where we stacked its mail bags. First Recon, 155 Howitzers, Thirteenth Motor T, each unit at Phu Bai had a mail orderly who would sort the mail further down by platoons or companies. Letters would be sorted into pigeonholes. When the holes were filled we would band the letters and toss them into the mail sacks near the throwing table. The throwing table was used for packages. Orange mail sacks were hung on racks in a horseshoe formation around the table, each with a nameplate. One or two men would throw the packages from the table into the right sacks. We didn't switch jobs very often, that way we increased our speed. When you had forty pigeonholes to sort mail to, after a few days you began to memorize their location on the box. Soon you automatically knew that First Force Recon was located in the lower right-hand corner, Thirteenth Motor T in the middle, Headquarters Company on the top row. Sort a few hundred letters a day and pretty soon your hands are flipping letters left and right, while you're jamming to the "Temptations" on Armed Forces Radio.

One day after work I walked across the barren compound. I looked at the hills to the southwest. The red dirt reminded me of south-central Oklahoma. For an instant I thought about crow hunting near Fort Cobb. How my friends and I hid in the red ravines in order to ambush a few of the millions of crows that wintered there.

I stepped into my hootch and stripped. Towel in hand I walked to our showers, which were just pipes, no shower head. As luck would have it there was no water pressure. The Army had an old water-barrel shower nearby so I strolled over to it and hung my towel on a nail and stepped in. I turned the valve . . . no water. I swore under my breath and walked back to my hootch, forty yards away. As I reached the first step I heard a noise in the air and suddenly the shower barrel exploded, sending debris fifty feet in the air.

"Incoming! Incoming!" someone shouted, and Marines were running in all directions. I stood frozen, watching the pieces of wood and metal floating down from the sky. If there had been water in that barrel I would be dead. The pounding of rockets and mortars into our area broke the trance. I grabbed my weapon, ran to our bunker, and dove in as a rocket landed close by. My feet were bruised from running across rocks barefoot, but I never felt a single rock. Soon the bunker was filled with Marines, and our sergeant and the other guys started laughing at me.

"Hey, Vince, your eyes are big as saucers," Sergeant Binder said as sweat poured into his eyes.

"Hell, I was thinking of my girl, my folks and apple pie and Chevrolets," I said, while the guys laughed amid the explosions.

"Welcome to Nam, Vince. You're baptized now, son," Binder said.

The mortars walked their way to the airfield, we could hear their crump . . . crump . . . crump far away, so we emerged from our bunker. I couldn't walk, so Price and Jackson, a black corporal, carried me to my cot. I'd be okay in a day or two, I just had some bruises . . . it sure could have been worse. I sat on my cot thinking, somebody up there likes me . . . Wayne if it's you, you're doing a fine job. Sergeant Binder stopped in the next day, "Vince, the CO isn't going to let us give you a purple heart, since you didn't bleed or anything . . . " I stopped him, "Sarge, I don't want a purple heart, why if my mom got the news that I had been wounded it would just kill her, ya know what I mean?" We looked into each other's eyes. "Yeah, son, I know what you mean," he said softly, then he stood and walked away.

Two weeks passed, all was quiet. We hadn't been hit since my baptism. The sun was starting to set as Price and I walked along the dusty road that led to our hootch. Suddenly rockets were landing all around us and we dove into the shallow ditch that ran alongside the road. I raised my head just in time to see a Jeep with four Marines zigzagging down the road. Then the Jeep exploded . . . a direct hit. A short time later the barrage eased up. Price and I ran over to the Jeep. Nothing was left that even resembled a human body. Just then we heard someone calling for a corpsman. We walked over to the head and saw three dead Marines lying face down on the floor, all with wounds to their heads and bodies. A nearby truck showed the raw power of the shrapnel. Its sides looked like a sieve. Some holes were the size of a thumbnail, others were the size of a Zippo lighter. I'd seen what shrapnel had done to a human body.

As we stood there we saw two Phantom jets. They strafed the hills to the southwest, and a huge ball of fire rose from the hills. We cheered as the Phantoms screamed toward us, flying low across our camp. I'll never forget that pilot's face as he came by at treetop level. He had a big grin and a huge handlebar moustache. He gave a thumbs-up sign as he passed, then rolled his aircraft four times and screamed into the clouds. The second Phantom did the same.

Three weeks later the Marines pulled out of Phu Bai. We headed down south, to Da Nang. Three hundred twenty days to go. I don't know when the change occurred, but sometime between that first rocket attack and Da Nang my fear left me. I was concerned, but I just never worried about dying after that first time. I accepted the fact that I might not get back. We stayed in Da Nang a few days and I wrote Cindy and told her I was safe. Price and I tasted our first cold beer in months. We staggered back to our hootch singing "We gotta get out of this place," the unofficial national anthem of Americans in Vietnam.

Five days later I was assigned to Camp Lane, ten miles west of Da Nang. I worked with a Sergeant Beach and Lance Corporal Tony Paul. They were both Yankees . . . oh, great. It was a small unit located in the center of the camp. We sold stamps and money orders, and handled certified and registered mail. At the end of each day we ran our balance sheets, which meant a complete inventory of all cash and stamps on hand. We also sorted mail to units, and in the mornings we took turns making the mail run into Da Nang. The job was easy enough, but I didn't like the duty. It was boring. Paul and I didn't get along, and Beach was the quiet type.

I did like the base chaplain. Chaplain Martin was fifty years old, he had a broad smile and a southern accent you could hear a mile off. He was a fine man and a grandfather to boot. He'd show us photos of his wife and family. He and his wife were a handsome couple. I couldn't comprehend the dedication he had to serve his country. He should have been home taking his grandchildren to the circus, or going on a picnic with his wife, anything but being over here giving comfort to these kids. I respected his endeavor.

It was November when I received word that Cindy and her father had been killed in a car accident. I couldn't work and I asked Beach for the day off. I sat on the bunker that night looking up at the millions of stars in the sky and asking myself why Cindy? I was the one in a war, why not me? I stopped counting the days, I didn't care anymore.

December arrived and Mom sent me a genuine aluminum Christmas tree with all the decorations. I donated the tree to Chaplain Martin for his Christmas service. The grunts from the Twenty-sixth Marines needed that tree more than I did. Christmas Eve came, the chapel was packed and nearly two hundred dirty Marines stood outside. Paul and I sat atop our bunker that night eating Spam and a dozen of Mom's tortillas. Days later Chaplain Martin was killed. I felt so useless. I had joined the Corps to get revenge and all I could do was sell stamps. I asked for a transfer to a grunt unit but the captain denied it. I spoke with Sergeant Beach.

"Tell ya what, Vince, the divvy PO goes out on sweeps and guards the airfield whenever there's a red alert. That's about the only action in our field."

"I'll take it, get me out of here."

"I'll go down to divvy and see what I can do."

Two days later I was on my way. I felt good as I headed for the division post office. It had to be better than what I'd been doing. I felt like I wasn't doing my part. Men and boys were dying every day. Some lost limbs, others lost their eyesight, and there I was throwing mail. I felt guilty. I checked in with Gunnery Sergeant McArthur. He assigned me a hootch and told me that I would be working the directory section. I would be in the second platoon under the command of Sergeant Tuller. I dropped my gear on an empty cot and began unpacking. Soon a few guys came over and introduced themselves. I met Tom O'Malley from Boston, one hundred eighty days. He looked just like Howdy Doody. Rick Sposato from New York. "Call me Fat Cat," he said. He was six feet tall and well over two hundred fifty pounds. His round face was covered with zits, and his sweaty black hair stuck to his scalp. I could see rolls of fat through his green T-shirt. Ted Jenkins (T. J.) was a slim, nice-looking cowboy from Laramie, Wyoming. He had blond hair and blue eyes.

"Hey, Vinny, let's go to chow," Fat Cat yelled.

So he and I and T. J. went to the Air Wing mess hall. They showed me around afterwards, pointing out the PX, chapel, and sick bay, then we returned to our hootch. Fat Cat and T. J. went on to work at the post office as the day shift returned to the hootches.

The next morning we stood in formation and we listened as Captain West informed us that the amount of mail was too great for the number of men we had. I glanced at the first platoon. They had sixty men, and we had sixty men. He spoke on.

"Men, we're going to have to put in some overtime in order to get this mail to the troops. We will continue with three shifts, but we will be working sixteen-hour shifts starting today. We will continue working at this pace until I feel that we have made sufficient progress. That is all."

We were dismissed and I reported to the directory section of the First Marine Division Post Office. The directory section was in one corner of a large metal building that measured one hundred fifty feet square. There were ten of us on day shift. The directory books were alphabetized. In each book the person's name, rank, serial number, and unit were typed on tiny cardboard strips. If the individual had returned to the United States, he would have CONUS (continental United States) typed on his strip, along with the base where he was stationed if that information was available. If he was dead, then KIA (killed in action) would be placed on his information strip, if missing, MIA (missing in action) would be typed in. Beside each directory book was a large orange sack of letters sorted alphabetically to match the directory. In addition, sacks of unsorted letters and packages made a stack ten feet high, fifteen feet wide, and fifty feet long. As I looked at the mail to be worked I rolled my eyes. Gunny Mac (McArthur) smiled at me.

"Do you think you can get this mess out of here, Corporal?"

"No sweat," I replied, and the old gunny laughed and slapped me on the back as I took a seat at one of the directory books. We worked hard and fast, but the onslaught of mail continued. The days weren't bad, but at night Charlie would fire rockets into Da Nang, and some of them landed close to our compound. We never knew when one might drop in our lap.

One evening as Tet (the Vietnamese New Year) approached we were called to formation. I was a fire team leader in the fourth squad of the second platoon. We were told that we were confined to our compound. We were on alert status. No drinking was allowed in the hootches, if we were called we would have to move out fast. Then by squad we were issued more ammo and grenades. I was curious to see how much all this gear weighed: flak jacket, helmet, canteens, ammo, grenades, rifle, and bayonet. T. J. and I walked over to the freight scales and I stepped on with my gear. I weighed a whopping two hundred fifty pounds. I stripped off everything except my fatigues and boots, then stepped back on the scales. I weighed one hundred fifty pounds.

Four hours later, toward the end of our shift, we heard the sergeants yelling, "Saddle up, saddle up! We're moving out! Move! Move!"

Marines scattered in all directions, hustling to their bunks to grab their gear and then to formation. Captain West told us that we would be a blocking force for a sweep that was to begin at midnight. We boarded large trucks and rumbled out of Da Nang. We didn't go very far. The last mile was traveled without the truck lights, we got off in the dark and started out in single file. I had no idea where I was, but I didn't like it. Those guys made too much noise. They'd never heard the word "sneak." Canteens were sloshing, rifles banging on flak jackets, and guys muttering, "Watch that barrel!"

"Hey, fuck you!"

"Fuck you too!"

"Shut up!"

Somehow we made it to our blocking point without getting slaughtered. We split up. The first platoon went one way and we went the other. We spread out at twenty-yard intervals, Fat Cat and I wound up on the very end. We found a shallow ditch and crawled in. We were about ten yards from a twenty-acre rice paddy. A small village was on the other side of the field, maybe three hundred yards away. Fat Cat started talking shit, "Hey, Vinny, if anything happens . . . "

"Shut up, Cat, there ain't nothing gonna happen."

"Yeah, but . . . "

"Knock it off, Cat!"

"Okay, Vinny, okay."

We lay there for what seemed like hours. Fat Cat was chewing the shit out of his unlit cigar. Then Cat and I saw them at the same time. I flicked off the safety of my weapon and he did the same. The two shadows were two hundred yards away, coming straight for us. I crawled off and found Sergeant Tuller and we crawled back to Fat Cat. We were joined by Staff Sergeant Adams. Adams was a jerk, I had known him at Phu Bai. Tuller was an ex-grunt, but Adams pulled rank on him so that he could fire the flare. The idiot fired the flare low, almost taking off Fat Cat's head in the process. It landed in the rice paddy and lit up the two shadows, but it lit us up as well.

"Who goes there?" Tuller yelled.

Then one of them yelled back, "Hey, are you guys Marines?"

"Yeah, come on."

They didn't come, and we could hear them talking low, then one of them yelled, "Hey, where are the Cubs from?"

"Chicago, stupid!" Tuller answered.

The two Marines came running. The sweeping force had been ambushed, everyone had scattered, and luckily these two boys had run into us. We stayed put until sunrise, then we returned to the compound.

That was my first real adventure in Nam, and I relished it. Of course, I hadn't been shot at yet. When I did get shot at and saw my buddies fall, I grew angry, the warrior within erupted. Two days later Tet of 1969 arrived. The fighting continued. I performed well under fire, the acrid smell of gunpowder invigorating my adrenalin. Old Man Martin gave me the name Mangus, short for Mangus Coloradas, the famed Apache warrior. All he said to me was, "Mendoza, you're crazy!" I felt protected, much like my ancestors who had had medicine made to protect them in battle. I had that feeling, or maybe it was the spirit that was protecting me. I cheated death three times in Nam and I got my revenge for Wayne, but I felt empty inside. The taking of life even in war did not sit well with me. The thirst for revenge which had been my Holy Grail fell by the wayside. We only had a few days of combat. It was more than enough for one lifetime.

April arrived and I had been promoted to sergeant. I was assigned duty on board the U.S.S. *Sanctuary*. Once again I had that feeling that spirits were watching over me. For the first time in nine months I felt really safe. Gunny Mac and I looked at the mess that the Navy said was a mail room. It looked like someone's attic. Two weeks later I had order restored on the hospital ship. I had records of all the wounded on board, when they arrived, their outfits, and the dates they would be released. It was the least I could do for these Marines.

I'll never forget the first ward I entered. I started calling out names, and the looks on those kids' faces were worth a million dollars. Letters from home, letters from the world, letters that eased the pain and brought a smile.

"Hey, Sarge, anything for PFC Reed from Phillips, Wisconsin?"

"How about Lance Corporal Stubbins from Roth, Iowa?"

It was sometimes hard to enter the wards. Some of the kids couldn't talk, they could only motion to me. Others had tubes in their noses or tubes coming out of their throats. Some were blind and their buddies read their letters to them. What a waste of America.

One day we were headed up north to pick up wounded from Quang

Tri. I stopped and talked to a cute little Vietnamese boy. He limped, he would always limp. "Hi, partner," I said.

"Hi, Marine."

His two front teeth were missing, and his eyes sparkled. I talked to him in pidgin Vietnamese and he spoke to me in pidgin English, then he was on his way with the other children. Kids would always suffer in war. I grew sad as I remembered the ten kids at the Phu Bai dump who had been mistaken for Viet Cong. A machine gunner had opened up on them in the dark as they came through the wire. They were hungry and were only trying to get to the fresh trash. When we arrived the young Marine gunner was still crying.

I had another job on the *Sanctuary*. I helped carry the wounded to surgery from the choppers that landed on board.

"Choppers! Choppers! Man your stations!"

We would carry the men into the operating room and place them on the tables. From then on they were in the hands of the Lord and the best damn surgeons in the world. I can't say enough for those guys and the nurses. They were super! Carrying the wounded took some getting used to. You gave one hundred ten percent. Seconds count between life and death. The look in those kids' eyes as they look at you for help. They grab at you with their hands as they fight the pain. They hold on to you and grit their teeth. All the while you tell them, "Hold on, man, you got it made now. You're gonna make it!" Sometimes they make it, sometimes they die in your arms.

As the last chopper of the day left, I stood outside the operating room. I lit a cigarette and turned away from the chaos of the busy room. I looked out at the ocean and cleared my mind of the screams and moans of the wounded. I don't know how long I stood out there, but when I turned around the operating room empty except for one body that lay fully clothed on a table. I slowly walked over to the body. I couldn't take my eyes off his face. His eyes were open and his mouth was open and twisted, as if in a silent scream of rage at having his life snuffed out. I stared at his eyes, eyes that stared blankly in death, eyes that looked deep into my soul. What had those eyes seen in the last seconds of life? What had they seen in his short lifetime? His arms were bent at the elbow and his fingers were spread wide and bent. Rigor mortis had already set in, he must have been dead when they brought him aboard. We were about the same age, he was white, with brown hair. He was covered in mud. I didn't look for the wound that had taken his precious life, I just looked at his face. He had loved ones that would forever miss him. Maybe a son or daughter that would never know his smile or touch. I felt my eyes water as I said a prayer for the young boy. It was the only prayer I knew. I had said it every night of my life until I reached the age of thirteen. I knew that God would know that this prayer was for the boy. "Now I lay me down to sleep . . . "

It felt good to be back on the ground as I thumbed my way through Da Nang. When I returned to the compound it was like old home week. Ben Humphries, a black corporal, opened his prized bottle of Chivas Regal in honor of my return. Ben was a nice, soft-spoken kid from Alabama. We had talked about life back home and the prejudiced people we had tolerated there. He seemed surprised when I spoke of my problems being Mexican and Indian. He paused a moment as we sat on the steps to our hootch. "Can I ask a favor of you, Vince?"

"Sure, Ben, shoot."

"If I get killed, would you write my girl and my mama for me?"

"Sure, Ben, no sweat man."

"I got another favor to ask."

"Yeah, what's that?"

"I know this sounds stupid." He paused, "Can I touch your hair? Man, I ain't never seen such straight hair as yours."

I laughed and lowered my head as he reached out his black hand and playfully rubbed my hair, "Oh, man that's weird!" and I raised my head and said, "My turn." I rubbed his woolly head, and dust flew, "Man, you feel like a sheep," and we laughed together.

I looked at the other guys as Ben took the first chug of Scotch and passed it to me. I drank, then passed the bottle to John Martin, a wacky draftee from Four Corners, Maryland. The "Old Man," as we called him, had qualified in boot camp for Officer Candidate School. College educated, he told them that he didn't have time for their silly war, he had better things to do than get a bunch of kids killed. I was the first Indian he had ever met, and he was taken with me. He kept us in stitches with his antics. Next to the Old Man sat Tommy Jones, a clean-cut kid from Ohio. I had named our platoon the Buffaloes, since we were fast and mean. Tommy would walk about daily chanting in a gruff voice, "Buffalo, buffalo." Next to him sat Ron Champlaines, from Kentucky. He was barely twenty years old and married. His daughter had been born while he was in

Nam. He had a Kentucky accent, which is a lot different from a Deep South accent, and everyone liked to hear him talk. The last kid in our group was David Graham. He was quiet and of medium build with sandy brown hair and brown eyes. I always looked out for Davey. He was an orphan. He had no one at home, not even a girlfriend, I thanked God for my family. Each of us had footlockers with photos of loved ones arranged on them. Davey had a picture of a pretty blonde smiling. She was the advertisement that came with the frame, the price was clearly marked in the corner of the generic photo. I felt sad every time I looked at it.

We sat in the dark on our bunker passing the bottle around. We laughed and talked and sang along to "Hey, Jude!" as a million stars sparkled on the clear night.

August arrived. I was a short-timer. Seven days and a wake-up! I was walking across the compound when I heard someone call my name. I turned and saw Larry Price jumping down from one of our large trucks. I walked toward him smiling as he unloaded his gear from the truck. We shook hands and congratulated each other for surviving . . . we were going home.

Seven days later Larry and I checked into the transit facility, then we transferred over to the departure facility. The time was getting close. We were listed on the manifest to leave the next morning at nine o'clock. I lay in my rack trying to think how it would feel to be back in the world, which was our terminology meaning the United States. I wouldn't know how to act with a good night's sleep. Every night the rockets would land and I would go from a sound sleep to a sprint in less than a second.

That night six of us sat around our racks talking about food. One guy would say pizza, the next, spaghetti, hot dogs with mustard and relish, suddenly bullets tore through the plywood walls and guys started screaming and crying, "Not now, don't kill me now!" The Viet Cong had struck and then run back into the darkness. Luckily, no one was hit. We were unarmed except for a few sentries, and I didn't like it.

The next morning everyone was up bright and early. It was our time. We boarded the buses and headed for the airfield. We had waited a long time for this day. We got off the buses and that's when we saw it, the long, beautiful Continental Airlines jet. We boarded one by one, Chicanos, Indians, blacks, whites, we were all there and headed home. As we left the ground a loud cheer rang out. I looked down at the green landscape and the many rice paddies. I thought of Cindy and the irony of her death. Then I thought of Wayne. I got 'em, Wayne, I said to myself, it's done. Now it's my life, Wayne, but I won't ever forget you. Larry elbowed me in the side. He looked at me and winked. He didn't have to say anything. I smiled and sat back . . . I was headed home.

NINE // **Mi Familia**

On 26 February 1970, a memorable day, I opened the trunk of my 1969 Cutlass Supreme, my friends quickly loaded their seabags into it, and we cheered. John Martin, Tommy Jones, Ron Champlaines, and I had just received our military discharges. The pink IDs that we held in our hands proved that we were now ex-Marines. As we drove out the back gate for the last time everyone leaned out a window and waved his pink ID at the MP on duty. He promptly came to attention and then gave us the finger as we drove past him. We drove to a country western bar that we had called home for the past five months. We had spent so much money in that little place, the owner gladly opened the bar at ten o'clock in the morning for us. Our last night and this morning had been on the house. We had a few beers and shot a last game of pool, then it was time to leave. I drove to the bus station in Oceanside, California. We had already exchanged addresses and goodbyes, all that was needed was to unload the car. We shook hands for the last time and wished one another well. We would probably never see one another again. Each of us would begin a new chapter in his life. But we would always be young Marines in the buffalo platoon whenever we heard the word "Vietnam"; we would never age, and I—I would always remember Mangus.

All March I lay around the house. Mom, Dad, and Junior were all smiles. It felt good to sleep in. What felt even better was the thought of no more inspections or field days.

I began dating Debbie, the pretty blonde I had met at that dance during high school. Her marriage to the Army officer had been annulled after six months. The officer and gentleman already had a wife and family.

On my return from Vietnam I found that American women meant more to me than before. As a Marine I had taken them for granted. The war had changed all that. Now when I look at a woman, any woman, I remember what it was like without them. It was a terrible time. Now I see them as delicate and yes, to a point, innocent, for they have not seen the carnage that we witnessed in war. Their love is to be cherished and honored. Maybe that is why our parents had such good marriages. World War II had made our fathers realize what they had. The same holds true for children. I had seen what war could do to a child. Now when I see any children I pray to God that they will never know the horrors of war.

April arrived, and after taking the civil service exam for the postal service I found work at a local steel company. The job was dirty and paid minimum wage, $1.90 an hour. Young and in shape, I welcomed the manual labor. It was a far cry from the gravy job that I'd had in the Corps. Debbie and I saw more and more of each other. The thought of marriage crossed my mind. It would be nice to have someone to come home to. I was tired of the bar scene. Chasing women and catching one now and then, bar fights and hangovers seemed to hurt a little more than they did before. I didn't think of college. If I hadn't met Debbie I might have gone. Many a good man has been bitten by the love bug, I was no different. By the end of April I had interviewed for a job in Dallas working as an assistant manager for a cafeteria chain. On 6 May 1970 Debbie and I were married in Sand Springs, Oklahoma. We didn't have a honeymoon, we spent our wedding night at the Mayo Hotel in downtown Tulsa. The floor that our room was on was also hosting a women bowlers' convention. They were having a grand old time when Debbie and I arrived . . . they would have made good Marines. They knew we were newlyweds by the corsage and boutonniere that we wore. When the champagne arrived, they were trying to peek into our room as if Elvis himself were inside. After room service left, a dozen drunken ladies stood outside our door singing "Moon River." We laughed, then we finished our champagne.

The next day we set out for Dallas, a small trailer in tow, and arrived just in time for the five o'clock rush hour. It was my first experience with heavy traffic. Dallas drivers are . . . let's put it this way, if you can drive in Dallas during rush hour you can drive anywhere in the world! Debbie had worked for a national insurance agency in Tulsa and had transferred to the Dallas office. We were all set to begin our new lives.

My hours were long and hard, sometimes seven days a week. I worked with mostly blacks, a few whites, and a Mexican woman. I liked the blacks; they were good workers and good people, we got along just fine. One day I was out on the lines exchanging empties for full pans of hot food when I heard yelling in the kitchen. I hurried to the kitchen and to my surprise I saw Jimmy, a black who was about my age, with a butcher knife in his hands, he was mad and cussing a blue streak at one of the new managers. The young manager was tall, heavy set, with red hair. His eyes were as big as saucers. He was scared to death. Everyone was standing around doing nothing so I quickly stood in front of the scared manager. I was thinking of Jimmy. He was a good guy, I couldn't imagine what had set him off.

"Jimmy, man, put the knife down," I said.

"Get out the way, Vince, I'm gonna cut him!"

"Jimmy, he's not worth it, man, you don't want to do time. C'mon, what did he do, Jimmy?"

"The motherfucker touched me, he grabbed me! Wanted me to do something, so the honkey motherfucker grabbed me! Ain't nobody ever grabs me!"

"He's not ever gonna grab you again, are you?" I asked the frightened manager over my shoulder.

"No, no!"

"C'mon Jimmy, give me the knife." I took a step toward him and I saw him slowly lower the knife, his eyes still glaring as I reached out for it. I stopped and turned to face the manager.

"I think you owe Jimmy an apology."

"I'm sorry, Jimmy, I wasn't thinking, I'm really sorry, it won't happen again."

That satisfied Jimmy and he handed me the knife. The others all went back to their business and I walked Jimmy over to a prep table.

"Jimmy, you can't be doing this stuff, man. If you had cut him you would have ruined your life. You're too smart for that."

"Aw, them managers are always looking down their noses at us."

"Look, if you go to jail the whites win. You can be black and be proud, but don't let ten seconds of angry get you ten years of hard time, man." Jimmy nodded his head, "Yeah, you right. That white tub a shit ain't worth ruining my life. Thanks, Vince, you're all right."

As minorities, we all carried invisible scars; I couldn't stand by and watch Jimmy go to jail because of pride.

Debbie and I drove back to Tulsa whenever I happened to get a weekend off. We drove her new Fiat Spider convertible. Like her father, energetic and self-confident, she never met a stranger. We had nothing but fun together. When we couldn't get away to Tulsa we would go to Six Flags and just enjoy being together. In November we moved out of our one-bedroom apartment to a two-bedroom rental house that she was crazy about. It was nice having a yard. By December we were thinking about starting a family. The thought of being parents thrilled us. We would lie in each other's arms and talk about naming our first child.

In February 1971 we returned to Tulsa. Dallas had been no more than a concrete jungle to us, every morning we would read about someone being shot or stabbed in Dallas. I was glad that Tulsa wasn't like that. We returned to our beloved Oklahoma. We would raise our children in the safety of our home state. I found work at a plastics company in south Tulsa. Cousin Butch worked there also, and I was glad that we could work together. Like most relatives we usually never saw each other unless someone died. Debbie was able to transfer back to her company's Tulsa office. We rented a two-story brick house near Fourth and Yale. It was at this house that Debbie told me she was pregnant. We were delirious with happiness, and Debbie never looked prettier. I had pep in my step once again, I was going to be a daddy. I even whistled as I left for work.

My job was to mix fiberglass with several different resins, from there the liquid plastic would be poured into molds. One day, just as we broke for lunch, I was walking down an aisle when I saw several men gathered around an unconscious girl lying on the floor. I figured she didn't need any further assistance so I continued toward one of the exits. Butch and I always ate lunch together out by a shade tree in the parking lot. I was almost to the door when suddenly fifty men came running out of the shop, passed me, and jammed the doorway with bodies. "Fire, Fire!" someone yelled and I looked around. I saw two men trying to open an overhead door that was locked. Six other men and I ran to their assistance. We broke open the door and desperate men ran for safety. I looked back over my shoulder and to my horror I saw Butch trying to carry the unconscious girl. He had his elbows under her arms and was half-dragging her as smoke and flames closed in. In his right hand he still carried his sack lunch. I sprinted to Butch and the girl. As I scooped her up in my arms, I yelled out to Butch, "You could have carried her if you had dropped your lunch."

"Are you crazy? I'm hungry!"

We ran out of the building as the flames were about to close in around us. I carried her a hundred yards and then laid her down in the grass. She was breathing, but her skin was clammy, I knew that she was going into shock. I yelled for someone to bring a blanket. I elevated her feet and covered her with the blanket. Then the first fire truck arrived. The flames were spreading and Butch and I ran to my car. The keys were in my jacket inside the inferno, so together we pushed it out of harm's way. As we were walking back to where the girl lay, a fifty-five-gallon drum exploded. It sounded just like a rocket attack. Butch and I dove for the ground. As we hit the ground we looked at each other and began laughing. Our reflexes from Vietnam were still with us. We stood and turned to look at the raging fire. Fifty-five-gallon barrels were shooting fifty feet into the air. Butch was the real hero. He had seen the flames erupt near the men and the girl. The men had dropped her and run as the flames surrounded them. If Butch hadn't been there she would have died. We didn't even know her name. We sat on the hood of my car watching the fire. Butch pulled a peanut butter sandwich from the sack. I looked at him with hungry eyes. "Where's your lunch?" he asked.

"In there."

He took a bite and mumbled with his mouth full, "Thith thure ith good." His eyes were dancing with orneriness. Then he reached inside his sack and tossed me another peanut butter sandwich.

Butch and I got a ride to my mother's house, later Debbie arrived from work in tears. News of the fire was on every radio station, they reported that several men were missing. Actually only one man died. I had the hair singed off my arms and minor burns. Butch and I never saw our co-workers again.

Spring arrived. I found a job with a large department store in Tulsa. I worked at their warehouse on the south side. Debbie and I began looking to buy our first house. We found a nice brick house near Ninth and Richmond. It had been on the market for two years and the realtor would not budge on the price. He called me at home and said he was sorry, but the owners were set on that price. Debbie was mouthing the words "take it, take it," and nodding her head. I declined. I apologized to the realtor for taking up his time and told him the best we could offer was $13,000. I hung up the phone. Debbie was frantic. "We can afford that, honey," she said. Just then the phone rang. I smiled and said, "That's him now." Debbie just looked at me.

"Hello, yes. Tomorrow at five, fine." I hung up the phone and looked at Debbie. "They accepted my offer." She screamed and jumped into my arms, I swung her around and around as we kissed.

We moved into the small two-bedroom house a month later. Debbie made a baby's room out of one bedroom, and of course we repainted the entire interior of the house. We were on top of the world.

In July, Arnold was home on leave from the Navy, so he and I went to play golf at a south Tulsa course. As we stood on the sixteenth tee a fellow in a golf cart approached us.

"Are you Vince Mendoza?" He asked.

"He is," Arnie said.

"Your wife is having a miscarriage. She's at Doctors' Hospital!"

Within minutes we were at the hospital. I rushed to the information desk. "Is Debbie Mendoza here?"

"Is she an OB?" The elderly lady asked.

I thought frantically. I didn't know what an OB was, "No, she's going to have a baby!"

The elderly lady and everyone within hearing distance laughed heartily. When she stopped laughing the lady patted my hand, "That means she's going to have a baby," she said still chuckling.

I hurried to Debbie's room. Mom was there with her. She was fine, she had started spotting and was frightened. She thought it best to go to the hospital just in case.

It was a September evening and Debbie and I sat in our den watching television. Her bag was packed for the hospital. A list of relatives' phone numbers lay on top of it. I had been the leader of an entire platoon of Marines in Vietnam. I was calm under fire, I kept my cool. This was a different situation. This was my wife and baby!

At two o'clock in the morning Debbie woke me, "Vince, Vince, I think it's time." When her words finally reached my sleeping senses I sprang from the bed with the speed of superman. I hit the floor running, where to I didn't know. I ran to the door, then remembered I didn't have any pants on. I raced back to the bedroom, Debbie sat on the edge of the bed in her nightgown. She sat in silence as I raced past her. I frantically pulled on my pants and my boots. I then realized I had forgotten to put on my socks. No time for socks now, I thought. I ran around the bed to help Debbie stand. As I helped her into her robe I was hopping up and down, my mind was racing. I threw on a shirt, not bothering to button it, then I raced down the hallway shouting, "I've got your bag, Debbie, I've got the bag!'' I grabbed the bag and list and ran out of the front door and to our car. I frantically searched for my car keys, and finding them I threw the bag in the backseat and then jumped into the driver's seat and started the car. I've got everything, I said to myself. I put the car in reverse and backed down the driveway. As I backed out into the street I looked toward the house. There stood Debbie on the front porch with her hands on her hips.

Two days later, on 17 September 1971, Felicia Ann Mendoza was born. Like all Indian and Mexican babies she was born with a full head of black hair. When I first saw her I was amazed. This little girl came from our love. She had the correct number of fingers and toes, she was ours, and I was a daddy.

Mom and Dad were on cloud nine. They had a new granddaughter. Ron and Linda had moved to Chicago in 1967, so the only time my folks saw Diana and Kevin was at Christmas and on vacations. Now they would have a baby in town to visit.

Oscar and Julie, Debbie's parents, had sixteen grandchildren, but since Debbie was the baby of the family her baby was special to them. Oscar and I stood staring at the baby. We had named the baby after him and Julie, Oscar Fleece and Julia Ann. Tears came to his eyes as he looked at Felicia. "I wish my daddy could see this baby."

"He can," I said, and the old man smiled and slapped my back.

Spring arrived and with it came strange happenings at the house on Richmond. I first noticed that every time we returned home from visiting friends and relatives a light would be on. Finally Debbie and I went through the entire house and made sure that all the lights were off when we left to visit our parents. When we got home the kitchen light was on. Each weekend a different light would be on when we returned. Debbie, like me, believed in the invisible world. I had told her the stories that I'd been told, and I told her of my seeing Joseph Smoke. One morning at breakfast I saw something flash by me, I looked quickly to my right, Debbie saw it too. "Did you see that?" she asked. I nodded my head.

"I wasn't going to tell you, but last Saturday when you played golf I heard someone talking to the baby in her room. I thought it was you. When I walked into the room only the baby was there. All the doors were locked," she said.

"Let's not get jittery, maybe it will pass."

In March 1972 I was hired by Shell Oil Company in Tulsa. I started out in the mail room of the credit card center. It was an easy job, and I was happy with my life. We had benefits and that was an important part of our security. The people that I worked with were all very nice. Working with them was a pleasure.

In April we found out that Aunt Lucy had breast cancer. I hated the thought of Aunt Lucy suffering. She had always been so much fun talking and laughing. She and Mom had a hard life. Lucy was the baby of the family. She was divorced and taking care of her children the best she knew how. I felt so sorry for Butch, Brenda, Charley, Tommy, and Danny. When Aunt Lucy died in August 1972 I couldn't believe that God had taken her away from her children. She loved them so much. She needed them as much as they needed her.

With Lucy's death came a problem. Butch was working when he could find work. Brenda had room for Tommy and Charley, but she didn't have room for Danny at that time. We took Danny home with us right after the funeral. He was twelve years old and he liked staying with us. He had his own room (our former breakfast room), a desk for homework, which he hated, and new clothes. We took him with us to our church, Saint Luke's Episcopal, where he joined a Boy Scout troop. We had Christmas at Mom and Dad's house on Christmas Eve. At two in the morning I got up and placed two presents by our fireplace. One was a doll and one was an electric race car set. The next morning Danny knocked on our bedroom door. "Hey, Vince, somebody put two presents next to the fireplace."

Debbie and I looked at each other in mock surprise, "Well, it wasn't me," I said as we put on our robes and walked to the den with Danny. He stood in the doorway looking at the two presents. "I wonder where they came from?" I asked. Danny's mouth dropped open and we could read his mind. Santa Claus!

In April Brenda called to say she now had room for Danny. He was happy as he packed his bags, Debbie and I were sad. We would miss his laughter, and helping him with his homework. He was a lot of fun, and a lot of help around the house also. The day arrived when Brenda and her husband came by to pick Danny up. I was glad for him. He would be with his sister. He would return to the Indian way of life that he knew. He kissed Felicia and Debbie, and I patted his back as he stepped off the porch. Our house was quiet that night.

In August 1973 we moved to Sand Springs, Oklahoma. Slamming doors and footsteps in the house had become too much for our jangled nerves. We moved into a four-bedroom house not far from my in-laws. Debbie took a job at a bank in Sand Springs, and her mother babysat for us. Grandma Chelf always had children about. She had seventeen grandchildren, and there were always at least six kids at her house on any given day. She loved kids, the more the merrier.

On 20 June 1974 Micaela Mendoza was born. She looked exactly like Felicia, fair skin and a full head of black hair. She shared her birthday with Mom's brother Tandy and Grandma McIntosh. I really don't know how she ever learned to walk, Oscar and Julie were always carrying her. She was their last grandchild, and they loved her as if she were their first. Debbie had difficulty with her delivery. I could hear her screams from the waiting room. I would not put her through that again. My dreams of having a son were gone, but that was okay, I had two healthy girls.

On a cold Sunday afternoon in February, Debbie was talking on the phone in the living room with Mica lying on a blanket at her feet. I was watching a golf tournament on TV. Suddenly I saw Debbie peek into our bedroom from the hallway, then she looked into the den and saw me looking at her.

"Do you need something, Deb?"

"Oh no, no, nothing," she turned and walked back down the hall. I thought her actions were strange, so I stood and quietly walked behind her as she went back to her chair and picked up the phone. I stepped into the kitchen to listen. I couldn't believe my ears.

"Oh, yes, he's something. We've been seeing each other for a while. You know, drinks and things. No, he doesn't suspect anything."

I couldn't stand it any longer, I stepped from the kitchen and Debbie's face turned pale. She hung up the phone.

"Who were you talking to?" She told me the woman's name. "You told me she was nothing but a tramp!"

She jumped up from her chair and started screaming wild things at me, "I want to be pretty! I want men to look at me! I'm dying, I've got an incurable disease, and, and, I want to live while I can!"

We had more words and I stormed out of the house to cool down. I drove around for an hour or so, then returned home.

This was the first time I caught her, it wasn't the last. I couldn't believe that this had happened. I was crazy about her. I wanted her every minute of every day, and to hear her speak of another man crushed my world. If she wanted a divorce I'd give it to her, but I wouldn't file. I couldn't do that to my kids. I would not be the reason for them to be shuttled back and forth from home to home. No, I would be there for them. I would always be there for them. As far as Debbie was concerned I would never trust her again.

In 1976 we moved to a little house on Rawson Road in Sand Springs. It had almost an acre of land, the kids were growing and they needed room to run and play. We had a large garden and Deb and I worked in it every evening, growing everything imaginable. Winter came and we almost froze to death. We had an open-flame stove in the living room and heat from our kitchen stove, but the house was not insulated and the floor was chilly. Felicia lay curled up beside me on the couch watching TV.

"Felicia, if Daddy buys you a new house, what kind of house would you want? Two story or a big yard?" She looked up at me with her big brown eyes and said, "I don't care, Daddy, as long as it's warm." That almost broke my heart. I had some money saved in the credit union, and I told Debbie about it. She got mad and accused me of hoarding money from her. In a way I did, and I told her so. If I had money in the bank, it was never there long. I never deprived her or the kids of anything.

On New Year's Eve 1976 my father-in-law died. I really liked that old man. I couldn't have asked for better in-laws than Oscar and Julie Chelf. They were good country people, backbone-of-America people. He was the kind of man that would keep his word on a handshake, they don't make men like that anymore. He would always help those in need, he was that kind of man. I will miss Pappy forever.

Spring arrived and Felicia and Mica enjoyed swinging on the old tire that I had hung on a rope from a large elm tree in the backyard. The neighborhood children would come over and the yard would be filled with the shouts and laughter of children playing, and always running with Felicia and Mica was their tiny, black, curly-haired mutt named Weeny.

In July 1977 we moved into a pretty two-bedroom house near Twenty-Fourth and Yale. I'll never forget that date. I made the mistake of driving by the fairgrounds that day. Willie Nelson and Waylon Jennings and the boys were playing a concert at the fairgrounds, and there I was driving a big ol' Ryder truck and stuck in traffic. Living near the fairgrounds is not always convenient, especially when the fair is in town! Cars were parked on each side of our street for as far as I could see. Anyway, I smiled as I saw my new house with the "sold" sign in the front yard, then the smile disappeared when I saw a strange vehicle in my new driveway. I blinked my eyes and shook my head, the car was still in my driveway. I had remained cool and calm as I sat in traffic for over an hour between Fifteenth and Twenty-first Street, but now, now, now I had been violated! I cut loose with a string of good ol' Marine Corps swear words! My face was red, veins popped out of my neck, my eyeballs were banging the windshield as I yelled at the top of my lungs. I looked over at Debbie, froth dripping from my mouth. She had her arms folded in front of her with an "Alice Kramden" look on her face. "Now, didn't that do a world of good?" she asked matter-of-factly. I cut loose again as she sat looking at me. I walked to a neighbor's house and asked to use their phone. Twenty minutes later a beautiful tow truck arrived. The kind gentleman quickly towed the trespasser from my property, and I laughed and cheered as he drove away. I was soaked with sweat when I stepped into our new home. Debbie had the air conditioning on and the coolness sent a chill through me. She handed me a soft drink, "Here ya go, Ralph."

"What do you mean, Ralph?"

"You act just like Jackie Gleason in *The Honeymooners* when you go off!" she said, as she shook her head.

I thought a moment, then I slowly smiled, "Thanks."

Our new home was nice. The neighborhood reminded me of Beaver Cleaver's neighborhood. It was a long way from the three-room house on North Quincy. My children would be warm this winter, that was all that mattered.

The next few years were happy years. I was no longer in the mailroom. I was making good money working in the invoice processing department at the credit card center. It was a good clean job and I enjoyed my work. I made some great friends at Shell. We had company picnics, dances, golf tournaments, football games. The people in my department were all about the same age. So when school began we would take turns buying candy from one another, you know, for the kids' different fund drives. We were one big happy family, and we each knew everything about everyone else's personal life too.

Our family began attending Saint Luke's again. The children loved their Sunday School class, and I was elected to the vestry. Father Wilcox was near retirement and a young rector, Father Tom, sat in during the vestry meetings. He also conducted the Sunday services. One Sunday Debbie and I invited him over for supper. Of course Debbie was cleaning house all day, though it really wasn't that bad. She fixed her famous pork chops and rice, she warned the kids to be on their best behavior, as they looked at me I winked at them and they smiled. Father Tom arrived and we visited for a short while and then enjoyed a delicious meal. The children were on their best behavior, and Debbie was all smiles as we excused them from the table. We retired to the living room. Father Tom sat in Debbie's antique chair, I sat on the sofa to his right and Debbie sat on the loveseat to his left. We were comfortably talking about the church when suddenly Mica entered the room and stood before Father Tom.

"Hello, Mica, my dear. How are you?"

She was wearing a little pink chiffon dress, with white socks and pink leather shoes. She had just turned three years old a few days before. Quickly she drew her index fingers up to the sides of her eyes. She pushed them up, then down and as she did she repeated this verse, "Japanese, Chinese," then she pointed to her legs, "Dirty knees," then to our horror she pulled out her chiffon dress at the breast with each hand, "Look at these!"

Debbie's mouth dropped open and her eyes bugged out, and I must have looked like Ricky Ricardo as mine did the same. We were so shocked that for a moment we were paralyzed. But Father Tom wasn't.

"Whaaaat?" he asked. And before we could catch our breath Mica said it again, "Japanese, Chinese, dirty knees, look at these."

"MIIICCCAAAA!!!" Debbie shouted, little Mica giggled and ran from the room, leaving us to apologize to Father Tom who was laughing. He told us that Mica's verse was cute but even funnier were the looks on our faces.

I began playing Mexican music again with my friend Bobby Cervantes and his girlfriend Connie Hart. We played music all over the state, the largest dance was in Oklahoma City, to a crowd of two thousand people at the Myriad Convention Center. The most fun we had was at a summer house that Connie's parents, Beulah and Albert, had near Purcell, Oklahoma. When we arrived a small country band made up of teenagers was playing. Children were running about the farm, barbecue and watermelon were being served, it was an old-fashioned country gathering. We set up our amplifiers and some old-timers brought us "white lightning" and cold beer. We played from four in the afternoon until three in the morning. One old-timer said he had played with Bob Wills and the Texas

Playboys, and he complimented me on my sax playing. We played "Take Me Back to Tulsa" for him and Bobby added a funny verse, "She ran around the mulberry bush, I ran around to meet her. She pulled up her petticoat, I pulled out for Tulsa." We had a blast. Two weeks later I was talking with my brother-in-law Logan, and he said someone had told him that the best Mexican band they had ever heard had played for the best party they had every gone to, near Purcell. When I told him it was our band he just laughed, "Everybody in the county was talking about that party, it must have been something."

That fall I received a notice that the graduates of Central High, class of 1966, were going to have a party at an apartment complex on the south side of town. Debbie and I and another couple went to the reunion. I walked in and immediately saw my friends from high school. I greeted them warmly. I had thought of them when I was in Vietnam and wondered if I would ever see them again. They were cordial and pleasant, but they had changed. Most were college grads with well-paying jobs. All they could talk about was what they had bought.

"I bought Judy a hundred thousand dollar house overlooking Tulsa," one fellow boasted.

"Sandra and I each own a Porsche," another bragged, as if material things made them better people. They were strangers with familiar faces.

I saw some of my buddies from my junior high football days too. "Man, when I was in Nam, I sure thought about you guys a lot," I said, smiling. Jerry, who had been a good friend and now was a graduate of the University of Oklahoma, sneered at me and turned away, "I don't want to hear about it!"

I watched him walk away and I grew angry, and for a second I thought about punching his lights out. Then I calmed down, I felt sorry for the guy. I was glad that I didn't go to college if it was going to change me like it had my friends. I saw Steve Mulligan come in and went over to greet him. He looked at me and walked on by as if I didn't exist. What a jerk! I should have let the horses run over him that night of the campout. I stood and looked at the group of people talking. What a sorry lot they'd turned out to be. Then I saw her . . . Bonnie. She saw me too and waved from across the room. She hadn't changed a bit. We walked toward each other, neither of us taking our eyes off the other's face. We hugged and exchanged pleasantries. She was still pretty, it was so good to hear her laugh and see her smile. She had married the geek and was living in Tulsa. I saw

Bonnie look past me and smile. I turned to look, it was Debbie. I introduced them and stood listening as they talked. I heard Bonnie ask Debbie
where we had met and Debbie said during high school. Bonnie told Debbie that she must be mistaken because she was going with me in high
school. They both turned to look at me and Bonnie had murder in her
eyes. I whistled a little tune and looked toward the ceiling as I turned and
made my way to the bar. I returned with three drinks. By then her husband
had joined Bonnie. Norvel and I stared at each other never saying a word.
I whispered in Bonnie's ear, "Remember the night we fell asleep at the
drive-in." She laughed and I smiled at Norvel, his face was red. Afterward Debbie said, "You dated that! She isn't pretty at all." I smiled.
Debbie didn't think Olivia Newton-John was pretty either. That was my
first and last reunion.

Felicia signed up to play girls' softball the next spring. Although I had
no intention of coaching I found myself in the position of assistant coach.
To my surprise I enjoyed it. That first year was memorable. "Chrissy go
to left field, Valeska, center field, Tina right field." They all stood looking at me. I thought a moment, "Chrissy go stand by the soccer goal, Valeska go stand in that patch of clover, Tina go stand behind that ant-hill
over there." They all scurried to their positions. It was going to be a long
year.

The nine-year-olds did well that year. I was never harsh with them, or
Felicia either. I remembered my father, there was no way I would do that
to my child. Felicia developed into one of the best clutch hitters in the
league. She didn't know what pressure was, and I was glad. I always told
her, "Do the best you can, that's all you can do." The games that child
won in clutch situations amazed me. The next year the coach and I had a
falling out. He insisted on screaming and shaking the kids for their mis-
takes. That was it, I was finished with the guy. To my surprise the girls
quit the coach and asked me to be the head coach. I agreed and was never
sorry for that decision. I loved all those kids. Some of their parents never
came to a single game in the seven years that I coached them.

One little girl had so much drive and desire. She was skinny and wore
glasses, she had long brown curls and a sprinkle of freckles. Her name
was Valeska, she was my center fielder. Time after time she would catch a
fly ball with her face and come in crying with a bloody nose or lip. But in a
matter of minutes she would be back at her position ready to do it all over
again. One year when the girls were fifteen we had a heck of a ball game

going on. Kim was pitching the game of her life. She would do well as long as her father didn't show up. I knew how she felt inside. It was the bottom of the fifth inning, the last inning. We were winning 1–0, the Bixby Bandits had runners on second and third with two outs. Kim had walked the last batter. I called time, and walked out to Kim. She smiled and wiped the sweat from her eyes as I approached. I smiled at her, "Ain't this fun?" I asked.

"Yeah," she laughed, "this is great!"

T. K., our little catcher, came out to the meeting also. She had a dead serious look on her face.

"Smile, T. K., or your face will stay like that," I said. She smiled as she stood listening.

"Okay, Kim, this is my call. I want you to smoke three right down the middle. You've been throwing smoke all night. Let's get this child out and send her home to her Mama!"

"You got it, coach!"

The batter fouled the next two pitches off. Kim looked over at me. I smiled and nodded my head at her. She smiled back and then a serious look crossed her face. She threw a white blur at the plate and the batter smashed a long drive deep to center field. Valeska froze for an instant, then she was off like a shot. The base runners were off and running at the crack of the bat. It was like a movie where everything is in slow motion. The ball hung in the air forever as it sailed toward the chain link fence. Valeska was running as hard as she could. With a mighty leap she sprang into the air and stretched as far as she could. The white ball landed in her glove. The crowd went wild as the team carried Valeska off the field. Looking at her as she smiled and cheered, I saw again the determined little nine-year-old girl with the bloody nose that would never give up.

Mica played softball for Hoover Elementary. She was a natural. She could catch and hit, and she was blessed with speed. I treated her as I did Felicia. I never put pressure on either of our children. They did their best, that was all that I asked from them. Mica's best was awesome. While I was coaching Felicia and the rest of the Angels, Mica was there listening and watching. She shagged balls for the team, never complaining, she loved the game and being with Felicia's team. When Mica's first year of softball came she was years ahead of her friends.

I loved my girls, and like any parent I wanted the best for them. I always told them that they didn't have to be a nurse; they could be the doctor. They didn't have to be a stewardess; they could be the pilot. I also warned them about drugs, "No Mendoza had ever done drugs, and if they ever did drugs, they had better hope the police got them, and not me!" I loved my girls, they were my pride and joy.

Felicia came home from school one day, she was upset. Her class had read where harp seals were being killed for their fur. She wanted to know what she could do to stop the killing. I helped her write a letter to our congressman, James R. Jones. A week went by, then one day Felicia received a letter from Congressman Jones. He wanted to meet her and her classmates. He also informed her that he had sent her letter to the Canadian ambassador and had talked to him regarding the killing of the harp seals. Felicia was thrilled!

On 2 July 1980 Grandma McIntosh died from complications caused by her diabetes. She was the sweetest, most caring person I ever knew. The sacrifices she made during her life were immeasurable. The night before the funeral an all-night service was held. Six ministers from Indian churches in Oklahoma, who had known Grandma and Grandpa all their lives, sat at the front of the church. Deacons seated the visitors, filling the front rows first. Debbie sat on my left side, Linda, Mom, and Junior sat on my right. The first minister asked the congregation to stand and sing a Creek hymn. Listening to the song, I flashed back to my youth. I could see Grandma and Grandpa singing that song, and I took pleasure in the monotone sound as the men sang with their deep voices almost drowning out the women who sang beside them.

The ministers took turns preaching and speaking all night long. None were college educated, they preached from the heart. They did not have millions of dollars rolling in from television pledges, at best they all had jobs and preached the gospel on Sunday. They were good men, salt-of-the-earth men. At one point the minister spoke to the few white people, "Now we're going to sing a song in English for the white folks that are here. Turn to page 221." He started singing in Creek again, and Linda whispered in my ear, "What happened to the white folks' song?" We chuckled as the non-Creek-speaking people looked at one another and smiled.

The ministers spoke of whatever came to mind and rambled on for what seemed like hours. At times the seated ministers would fall asleep themselves, mouths open, or even snoring. The first minister spoke about stealing chickens as a youth. It was indeed a sin, he said, but his daddy had run off and he and his little sister and brother were starving to death. He did what he had to do to keep his family from dying. He felt bad about what he had done, that was when he decided to preach the word of the Lord.

It was almost midnight. The second preacher stood before us preaching the evils of liquor. I looked around. Three other Indian men were awake, everyone else had one or both eyes closed, including the other five ministers. I could hear children playing outside. I saw a boy's face in the open window behind the speaker. Suddenly the boy screamed as loud as he could. The ministers all jumped at once, as did the congregation. Everyone laughed as the ministers traded eyeglasses that had fallen to the floor. The speaker, after grabbing his heart, replied, "I see the Lord done sent one of his messengers to keep you backsliders awake!" Everyone laughed. We left at one o'clock in the morning.

In the Indian church the next day, the heat became unbearable. Sweat poured from everyone as the single fan blew hot air, the women fanned themselves with kerchiefs, and the men wiped their brows to no avail. They had put makeup on Grandma. Grandma never wore makeup, she looked odd with rosy cheeks and light skin. I thought of the time I took her for a drive in Debbie's green sports car. She wore her long black coat and her head scarf, in her mouth a dip of snuff. If the temperature was below 75 degrees she wore her coat and scarf. I had the top down on the convertible. It was her first ride in one. As I sped down Riverside Drive weaving in and out of traffic I would hear an occasional, "Mmmm-mmm," come from her direction. When I stopped the car in front of Mom's house Grandma let out a cackle of laughter. "My goodness that was fun! Mmmm, but you sho drive too fast," then she laughed again.

She was buried in her black shawl between Grandpa and Lucy. Tandy and Solomon rest just to the north of them. Grandma was with Grandpa now, and I could feel her love as we took turns with the spade covering her casket. I was thankful that our children were old enough to remember their great-grandmother.

In December 1980, as I drove home from the midnight shift at Shell, a news report came over the radio and my heart sank. A two-car accident with no survivors. Six Indians had been riding in one car, and the accident was just north of Okmulgee. I hurried home and called Mom. My fear was realized: my cousin Danny, his wife, and Butch's wife, Norma, were among those killed. They had all been out drinking that night. The driver, someone I didn't know, was driving on the wrong side of the four-lane highway at eighty miles an hour. They crashed head-on into an old man in his pickup. They died instantly. They were buried next to Lucy.

In April 1983 Debbie and I were having trouble again. She had been working for American Airlines since 1979. I didn't know if she was seeing someone there or not, but she didn't want anything to do with me. I moved out for two months. I felt out of place being alone. I didn't know what I had done wrong. I didn't bat an eye when she wanted a new Lincoln Towncar, I was content with my old pickup. Maybe I gave her too many material things. I gave her love, that was for sure, but maybe love was not enough.

It was during this period that I was unfaithful to Debbie. I felt strange walking into the dimly lit smoke-filled bar. I sat at the end of the bar and asked for a Seven and Seven. It was early on a Friday night. I looked about the bar at the mixture of people. I shook my head and asked myself, what am I doing here? I thought of Debbie, maybe I should have divorced her years ago, then I thought of the kids. No, I had made the right decision. By my third drink I was feeling relaxed. I saw an attractive brunette sitting with a dishwater blonde and I walked over and asked the brunette to dance. She declined, she was having boyfriend trouble and didn't feel like dancing. Her friend wanted to dance so I danced with her. She was tiny and slim, we hit it off, and she asked me to join them at their table. We left before closing time and I took her to my apartment. I felt guilty for being with another woman, then I remembered that Debbie didn't want me, and she had been with another man. That justified my actions. It was a shallow experience. There was no love in the act. Of course making love to Debbie might have been one-sided love on my part, I didn't care, I was crazy about her. If I had been single this woman might have been terrific. The sex didn't do a thing for me. Maybe I was screwed up in the head, men were supposed to nail everything that breathed. The more women they conquered, the more macho men became. I had been like that in the Corps, but now I only wanted my wife.

I continued my masquerade at the bar. By month's end I actually had women fighting over me, but that wasn't what I needed. I missed my kids. I missed my ho-hum daily grind life. I missed Debbie.

Mid-June arrived and I drove to my house to talk with Debbie.

"Do you want me to come home?" I asked.

"I really don't care, it's up to you."

"Do you really mean that?"

"I don't know."

If she didn't want me back, then it was over. I would file for divorce. I would survive, I would go on.

"Do you have anything you want to say?" I asked.

"No."

"Well then, I'm going to file for divorce, I can't live like this."

To my surprise she started crying, she dropped to her knees and grabbed my leg. "Don't leave me, please don't leave me. I was just toying with you. I don't want you to go. Oh God, don't leave me!"

Felicia and Mica stared at the scene from the hallway, then returned to their room.

It was over, this terrible episode of my life. Little did I know that this was just the tip of the iceberg. We are educated in basic math, history, and other subjects, some go on to college, but no one ever teaches us how to love, how to make a relationship work. We are abandoned and ignorant about the single most important aspect of life, the nurturing of a relationship. Each person is left to go it alone. Little did I know the worst was yet to come, that more stress and heartbreak would soon enter my life.

TEN // **The Awakening**

In July 1983 I sat at the dining room table with my checkbook and a stack of bills. The kids were watching television, Debbie was washing dishes. There was a knock at the door. It was Becky DeGraw. She and her husband Sonny had been neighbors, but they had moved away and this was the first time we had seen Becky in several months. We exchanged greetings, then I excused myself and returned to my stack of bills. I heard Becky tell Debbie, "Come outside and see my surprise." When they returned, Debbie was carrying a baby. Debbie and Becky continued to talk in the kitchen. Then Debbie walked over to me, still carrying the baby.

"Vincent, Sonny and Becky are divorced. Becky's working the midnight shift at the post office and she needs help, can we keep the baby for her until she gets on her feet?" I thought a moment, it was out of the question, I said, "No."

"Here hold him a second," she said, as she thrust the five-week-old into my arms. Then she turned and went back into the kitchen. I walked over to the couch and sat holding the baby, Felicia and Mica on each side of me. He was a cute little guy. I rubbed his chin with my finger and he grabbed it with surprising strength. I laughed and he did too. His eyes sparkled. I looked toward the kitchen, Debbie and Becky were peeking around the corner. "Oh, all right, we'll keep him. But just till you get back on your feet." Debbie and Becky hugged each other and the kids cheered. Little did I know that I would grow to love this child as if he were my very own son.

He slept between Debbie and me, arms and legs outstretched to touch both of us. We shared the two o'clock feedings, Debbie was in charge of the dirty diapers, I changed the wet ones. Months passed and little Lance Anthony DeGraw was crawling. He had blue eyes, blond hair, and a button nose. I was Da-da to him. Debbie and the kids called me Daddy, Bucky did too. I called him Sammy Buck, later I dropped the Sammy.

Buck was the son I never had. The entire family loved him, Mom, Dad, and Junior, everyone that met Buck fell in love with him.

By December 1984, Becky and Sonny were back together and came to Mom's house for Christmas. It was a happy occasion having the three of them there. We welcomed them to our family as if they were kin. Becky handed Lance a present and said, "Here, son, take this to Daddy." Lance toddled over to me and handed me the present, everyone laughed as Sonny said, "No, son, your other daddy," and everyone laughed again.

That first year with Lance we kept him every night, except on weekends. He was no trouble, we loved him as our own. The kids loved Buck, Debbie was crazy about him. Buck and I were inseparable from the beginning. He would crawl into my lap and I would show him pictures from my hunting magazines. Together we would look at deer, bears, and squirrels. Wherever I went in the house or the yard Buck was right by my side.

By the time he turned two he was smacking the plastic ball with the plastic bat. He was a natural, his hand and eye coordination amazed me. As we played together in the backyard I realized that something was wrong. I had set out bases for him to run after he hit the ball. He ran to first base, and started toward second, then he stopped. He bent over and held his stomach, pain crossed his face. I ran to him as he straightened up.

"What's wrong, son?"

"I hurt, Vince, my stomach hurts."

I picked him up and carried him to the house. That night he ran a high fever. When Becky came to pick him up the next day we told her about his pain and the fever. She took him to the doctor. They thought it might be a virus. A week later Buck was still hurting, and Becky took him back to the doctor. It was evening when Becky called. Buck had cancer. I thought I would die. I just had to go to a church to pray for my son. Debbie and I drove to Saint Luke's, it was locked. We drove downtown to Holy Family Catholic Church, it too was locked. Then I thought of Saint Francis Catholic Church where I had been baptized. We drove there. The front doors were locked, so I walked around to the south door, it was open. I signaled Debbie to join me. There was an old man sitting in a pew halfway back on the north side of the church. Debbie and I walked to the rear of the church and lit a candle. I placed two dollars, all I had, in the donation box. We knelt and prayed in silence. When we were about to leave, the old man started a conversation with me. I sat and talked with him about Buck. We said our farewells. I was about to go out the door when I turned to look at the old gentleman. He was gone.

Lance began chemotherapy immediately. We still kept him often for Sonny and Becky. I gave him a haircut, knowing that soon his hair would fall out. I did a terrible job, Monday morning when I saw him he was bald. "What happened to your hair?" I asked.

"My daddy threw it over the fence!"

I laughed out loud and Buck joined me as I hugged him.

The doctors had found a large tumor behind Buck's stomach. They gave him six months to live. I prayed night and day. The night before he was to have surgery, around two o'clock in the morning Sonny left Buck's hospital room to get a cup of coffee. Buck was sleeping soundly. When Sonny returned, the child was sitting up in bed facing a corner of the room.

"Lance, what are you doing up, son?" Sonny asked.

"Oh Daddy, there was this man with long white hair, and a long white beard. He was standing in a bright light. He said not to worry cause I was going to grow up to be a big boy!"

Goose bumps covered Sonny as he listened. They had never taken their son to church, how would he know about God, or angels? That morning Buck had surgery. Hours passed, then the doctor entered Buck's room.

"Mr. and Mrs. DeGraw, I can't explain this . . . the cancer is gone. The tumor was benign, all the blood work was checked and double-checked. There is no sign of cancer anywhere."

They kept Buck a week in the hospital. They checked his blood work over and over, still no cancer was found. It was a miracle! We resumed our lives, my son was well.

He still slept with Debbie and me. I would open my eyes in the morning, and there he would be, his face next to mine. He was so close that all I could see was blue eyes, then he would laugh and kiss me. The world was beautiful again. Sonny and Becky's work schedules allowed them to begin keeping Lance more, but he still stayed with us on occasion, and those occasions were special to us.

I started my own Mexican band that summer. It was a ten-piece group. I wrote the musical arrangements for the two trumpets and my sax. I didn't ask Dad to join, he wanted everything his way. No one else knew anything according to him. He looked over my arrangements one day, trying to find fault with them. He pointed out what he thought was an error. We didn't have a fight, but I told him he was wrong. That didn't set well with him, and he puffed up. I was not a child, I held my ground and told him how it was. The next day he phoned me and apologized. He admitted he was wrong. I bet that almost killed the old-timer, but he handled it well.

We played all kinds of music, rock-and-roll, country, mariachi-style, we even had a concertina player. Dad hated the concertina. He always said, "Only cotton pickers like that squeak box!"

My band lasted a year, then I called it quits. The dances were becoming brawls because of the "mojados," illegal aliens, "wetbacks" we called them. The first- and second-generation Mexicans were civil, but the mojados were out to make trouble. It was macho to fight at a dance, men or women, it didn't matter. Soon they began fighting with knives, the final straw was a gun fight on North Utica, not far from the Our Lady of Guadalupe Church. I would not endanger my family or my friends.

In 1986 Debbie quit her job at American Airlines. She was unhappy with her work. She wanted to open a Mexican restaurant. We shopped around before she quit her job, pricing restaurant equipment, which was almost equal to the price of gold. The markup was outrageous, but we went ahead with her dream. She took her savings and opened a small restaurant on Charles Page Boulevard, not far from Sand Springs. I still worked for Shell, while Debbie ran the business. She worked long hours, I helped when I wasn't working. After a year we were barely breaking even. She wanted a better location, but with that location would come higher costs, which could lead to financial disaster for our family. She moved the restaurant to Tulsa. I didn't like the location, but she was eager, she couldn't wait.

I had surgery in 1987 for diverticulitis. I was off work for six months. It was during this time that I decided to write an autobiography, the story of my joining the Marines. I called it "Adios, Tulsa. Hello, Vietnam." I wanted my children to know what Dad had endured as a young Marine. As I wrote my story I laughed out loud occasionally. The good times I'd had with my friends were pleasant memories. I wondered about my friends; were they doing well? I went on remembering the good old days, days when all I had to worry about was myself.

One day in July, Buck and I were coming home from Mom's house. Suddenly he sat down and began to cry.

"What's wrong, son, are you hurt?"

"No."

"Well then, tell me what's wrong."

"I miss my friend."

"What friend?"

"The man that came to see me in the hospital. The man with the white hair and white beard. I want to see him again," he said between sobs.

"You will, son, I promise, okay?"

"Okay," he replied, "I miss him, Vince."

I was surprised that he remembered the experience. My son and his friend had reinforced my faith.

I had returned to work by month's end. I was one of three lead operators in the inserting department at Shell, where automated machines stuffed advertising brochures into envelopes along with the monthly statements. We also handled payroll, vacation scheduling, work flow, postage meters, and month-end balance sheets. It was a good job, but it was a dead-end job. The supervisor positions were all held by people close to my age. In order to move up I would have to wait for someone to die or retire.

One night after Debbie and I closed up the restaurant, we sat and talked at the kitchen table. The restaurant was going under. She had tried to make ends meet by robbing Peter to pay Paul, but the overhead was too great. A decision had to be made. Unfortunately, in hindsight, it was the wrong decision. She had investigated the market for a tamale factory. She had taken her tamales to local distributors and they had all liked the product, but by Department of Agriculture regulations the tamales would have to come from a USDA-approved facility, which did not include restaurants. The only money available was the savings that I'd invested in the company. The only access to it was to retire or quit.

In August 1987 I quit my job at Shell. We had found a USDA-approved facility in Tahlequah, just a block from the campus of Northeastern State. In September I drove to Tahlequah. Once again I stared at the campus. I was forty years old, I would never realize the dream that had driven me to survive twenty years before. The students, now wearing loud colors and spiked hair, boys wearing earrings, passed on their way to class. My life had been a bounty of bad decisions. Deep in my heart I knew that this idea of a tamale factory was another. I couldn't say no to Debbie, her vigor and confidence, her winning personality, I loved her. I threw caution to the wind to please her. In doing so I failed her, and myself.

During September Junior and I drove back and forth from Tulsa to Tahlequah. We had fun working together and Junior liked being away from Mom and Dad. During that month Debbie closed the restaurant, and we moved to Wagoner, Oklahoma. We rented my cousin's house from his widow. We rented our Tulsa house to Debbie's sister. Debbie was the only one who did not like living in Wagoner. I had always wanted to live in the country or a small town. The girls loved Wagoner, and Junior and I were avid fans of the Wagoner Bulldogs football team. Felicia and Mica played fast-pitch softball for Wagoner High. They loved the small-town life, knowing everyone in town, they were all friends, and looked out for one another.

The house we lived in had been built by my cousin Joe, Uncle Claude's son. He had died from liver trouble just as Claude had. One day Felicia and Mica were lying in front of the fireplace doing their homework. Our Chinese pug, Heidi, lay between them. Suddenly Heidi jumped to her feet and stared at something invisible to us. She let out a low growl as the invisible being passed across the room, following the intruder with her head. We all watched her face as she continued to growl.

"It's okay, Heidi, it's only Joe. It's okay, girl, he won't hurt you," Felicia said. Mica smiled and nodded her head.

I was pleased. My children understood the invisible world. We Mexicans have always known that animals could see the spirits that walk among us. A week later Felicia told Debbie and me about the white mist. She felt it was Joe who had visited her. She was lying in bed looking out at the stars. Suddenly she saw something shimmering and white form at the foot of her bed. It did not take human form, it just floated in the air, but she saw two extensions come out from either side like arms reaching out. The floating form started toward her and she covered her head with her blanket. When she peeked out a few minutes later the apparition was gone.

It was autumn 1987. Felicia was a senior and Mica a freshman. Where had the years gone? I sat and looked at them as they browsed through a clothes catalogue together. They had been good children. Though they favored each other in appearance, they were as different as night and day. Felicia had been the perfect little girl, sweet and caring, love just flowed from her. Micaela was sweet and loving also, but beneath the sweetness was an independent child. Even as a toddler she made her independence evident. As she grew older she and Debbie had their differences, both being so much alike, neither realizing it. As a father I witnessed the ongoing soap opera discussions. "Where's my sweater?" soon to be followed by "That's *my* sweater!" And when Mica became a teen I joined the chorus, "Where's my T-shirt?" Mica was into baggy clothes and what better bags than Dad's colored T-shirts. When I came home from work one day, Mica and three little friends were just leaving the house as I pulled into the drive. They each had on a colored T-shirt. Naw, they couldn't be all mine, I thought. I hurried to my dresser and opened my T-shirt drawer. MMIICCAA!!!!!!

I did the fatherly tasks also. Either it was raining cats and dogs or there was an ice storm when I would hear the sorrowful lament from one of the three females in the house, "Dad! We need pads!" What greater sacrifice is there for a father to make. I knew the Lord was paying me back for my junior high days by blessing me with two bouncing, soon to be ovulating, little girls. Counting Debbie and Heidi, I was outnumbered four to one. I drove to the Quick Mart two miles away, sliding this way and that on the frozen county roads. It was a Sunday morning, the store was vacant except for a middle-aged woman at the register . . . it couldn't have been a male. I slowly prowled the aisles, my eyes searching for the feminine hygiene section. I looked around as I spied the embarrassing boxes, this was worse than buying a condom in a drugstore! I snatched the box and hurried to the register before anyone else entered the store. I grabbed a newspaper and a package of gum to throw off the woman at the register as to my mission. I looked out the front window as she tallied my items. She cleared her throat, then spoke, "Funny, isn't it?"

"What's that?"

"How women always run out of pads on this kind of a day."

I rolled my eyes, "Yes, it's hysterical," I said, and she laughed. I was starting out the door, when another man about my age entered the Quick Mart. He stopped just inside the doorway. His eyes clicked this way and that, then he slowly walked down the aisle . . .

In April 1988 I began working for American Airlines, while Debbie ran the tamale company in Tahlequah. Junior lived with us in Wagoner, he and Debbie would drive to Tahlequah daily while I drove the forty-five miles to Tulsa each day. I started out as a building cleaner at American. It was an entry-level job, but we needed the benefits and a steady paycheck. Six months later I became a stock clerk, with a raise in pay. I was on my way up the ladder.

We moved to Tahlequah that August. Junior became sick and returned to Tulsa to live with Mom and Dad. We leased a thirty-acre ranch northwest of the historical town. I bought a horse and Debbie bought a dozen chickens. We loved being in the country. I drove a hundred fifty miles, round trip, each day, it was worth every mile. Felicia was dating a real nice boy from Tulsa, Debbie and I really liked him. He was older than Felicia. He was intelligent, fun, and had manners. He was crazy about Felicia. To our dismay Felicia broke up with him a few months later. He was the only boyfriend of hers that I had liked, the others had all seemed a little weird.

On Labor Day 1989 we had a huge party. Friends and relatives came from all over to the outdoor cookout. Chidren were running everywhere, the old-timers played horseshoes, the teens played volleyball. Dad brought his golf clubs and enjoyed flogging the dirt on my thirty acres. I had cleared a picnic area within a grove of trees. I dug a pit and made a fire, we cooked a large pot of tamales on the fire. Ice chests were filled with cold pop and beer. Debbie's family brought fried chicken and potato salad for those who could not handle the spicy tamales. Junior played volleyball, he had a great time. We all laughed and enjoyed the afternoon.

The next day Debbie and I drove to Muskogee. We had declared bankruptcy because of the bills from the restaurant. Unknown to me, Debbie's sister had moved out of state, and no one was making our house payments. Debbie hid the mortgage company's letters from me until it was too late. We had lost our house in Tulsa.

The weight of the world was on my shoulders. Debbie had a bookie in Tulsa, how much she was gambling I did not know. More bills arrived, this time from the tamale company. I was home alone. I pulled my .357 Magnum revolver from the nightstand. I looked at the bullets in the chamber. Then I turned the gun and looked into the barrel of death. Why had I been spared in Nam? Others had died, why not me? Maybe I should die, sure, why not? I should have died on three separate occasions, why had God spared me? Debbie would be fine. She would remarry, the kids would have a new father. I thought of my little Buck. I couldn't leave him. How could I choose to deny my own blood of their father, and yet remain alive for Bucky? I couldn't destroy him. I couldn't leave him. I placed the gun back in the drawer.

On Sunday, 15 October 1989, Debbie and I were visiting some friends down the road. Our friends owned a tack shop and we were just standing around talking among the saddles and bridles when the phone rang. Debbie took the call. She handed the phone to me. Junior had died. I couldn't believe it. I was numb. We had discussed having Junior live with us after Mom and Dad died. It would be a hardship, but he was my brother. Now he was gone. He'd been sitting in his room watching the Dallas Cowboys, his favorite team. Mom and Dad were in the back bedroom, which they had made into a TV room, when they heard a thud. They hurried into Junior's room, he was already blue in the face. Dad began CPR, but it was too late. Junior had died instantly from a massive heart attack. He was forty-seven years old.

I stood alone at the funeral home looking down at Junior as he lay in his casket. I wanted to be alone with my brother. He was more than just a brother, he was my friend. We had almost died together once as we drove to work from Tulsa. We had just crossed some railroad tracks south of Wagoner in the fog when a train doing sixty miles an hour passed behind us in the dark. Junior's eyes were as big as saucers when I motioned for him to look behind us.

As I looked at him I remembered our fishing trips with Dad as children. The way he cried at sad movies. The trips that we as a family had made to Las Vegas. He loved Las Vegas. I touched his hands. Hands that could sign his thoughts to the world. Hands once nimble now lay still, rigid, silenced by death. I wanted to be with my silent brother. He had gone on without me. I signed the words, "I love you," then I lay across him and cried.

Mom and Dad were in shock. They had lost their oldest child. Dad bought three burial plots so that they would all be next to one another, just as they had lived their lives. The weeks following Junior's death I stopped by the house often before driving on to Tahlequah. The house was like a tomb. Dad would stand at the doorway to Junior's room and just stare. Mom sniffled and went about her housework.

November arrived. Dad and I talked of the coming deer season. He and I had hunted together every year since 1971. I hoped to take his mind off Junior's death. The Thursday before opening day he went in for a checkup. That night he packed his orange hunting suit, bedroll, and customized Mauser for opening day. Friday while he was at work Mom called him and told him the doctor wanted to check him into the hospital. He needed a heart bypass, how he had lived this long was a miracle in their estimation. We drove to Tulsa that night and visited with him. Saturday morning Sonny, Becky, and Bucky came by Mom's house. Bucky had an Indian headdress on, and a drum. He went with us to see "Grandpa," Dad was one of many grandpas to Buck. Dad smiled when he saw Buck, and the boy crawled up on Dad's bed and kissed him. Dad laughed and hugged him. Sunday evening was my last visit with Dad. His surgery was scheduled for Monday morning. Mom, Debbie, and Linda had left the room, Dad and I were alone. "You know son, when I get over this, I'm going to do things I've never done before."

"That's good, Dad, I think you should."

"You do?"

"You bet."

He smiled. I shuffled my feet, I knew it was time to leave. I looked at him as he lay there smiling at me. "I love you, Dad." The words surprised him. He reached up his arms to me, and as we hugged he said, "I love you too, son." It was the first time in my life that he had ever said those words to me. They were also his last words to me.

Complications arose during surgery. We waited for good news, but it never came. Wednesday morning at six o'clock, 22 November 1989, Dad died. It had been a dry fall, with no rain in the forecast. At the moment of his death it began to rain. I remembered the Mexican saying when someone good dies and it begins to rain, "the angels are crying." Aunt Connie and Uncle Joe were with us in the waiting room. Uncle Joe began to cry. We walked the slow walk to Dad's room. My cousin Ray walked with us. I was numb as I entered the room. I held Dad's hand. The hands that had brought such happiness to the Mexican colonia in Tulsa lay still. The sweet melody of his music was silenced forever.

Because of the Thanksgiving holiday Dad's funeral was not held until the following Monday. All his life Dad had wanted me to play his saxophone at his funeral. Mom always got on to him about it, "How can you ask him to do that? Don't you know how hard that would be?" But I owed that to him. He loved his music and I would honor my father's request. I walked to his closet and pulled the black case from its place on the floor. Which song should I play? Then I remembered the song the Mendoza family ended every dance with, "La Golondrina," the swallow. We called it the going-home song. And now Dad was going home. I stood in the closed-in back porch in the cold. I didn't want to disturb anyone as I practiced the pretty song. I would play a few notes, thinking of Dad, then I would break down and cry. I played Dad's song at the graveside. I could feel him with me, and I played the song perfectly. Linda said later that it sounded just like Daddy playing, and in a way it was.

Christmas was a quiet occasion that year. Dad had always passed out the presents. This year Ronnie took over the duties. I thought of Dad as I poured myself a drink in the kitchen. Dad and I had always shared a drink together on Christmas Eve. His life had amazed me. His family were poor migrant workers and coal miners. He had only gone to the sixth grade, but with his desire to better himself he sent off to a correspondence school and taught himself geometry and trigonometry. He did well and was hired by McDonnell Douglas aircraft. That was when we moved to our house on West Brady . . . my mansion. McDonnell Douglas had a shortage of experienced men in aircraft jig building. Dad was a member of the hand-picked team that was sent to Charlotte, North Carolina. Once in Charlotte Dad worked on the Hercules Nike missile project. He had come a long way from the coal mines of Oklahoma, loading coal for fifty cents a ton as a ten-year-old, to working on Nike missiles for his country. His remaining years he had worked at T.K. International in Tulsa as an aircraft parts inspector. The little man with the big desire was a success. My only regret was that I waited too long to tell my father that I loved him. I hope he knew all along.

Dad's death had an effect on Ronnie. Ronnie and Linda had always been good parents, and Christians. Dad's death brought an awareness of mortality to Ronnie and he became more compassionate. Ronnie and his daughter Diana shared a moment in Dad's TV room after the funeral. They held each other and cried. And as they held each other they exchanged the love that was in them for each other, bonding them closer than ever before. It was a beautiful sight, I could feel Dad's presence all about.

In February Ronnie retired from Borden's. He returned to Tulsa and stayed with Mom at her house on West Brady. In May, Linda and Ronnie bought a house in Tulsa. The need to be close to family was now his priority in life. Ronnie and Linda had left Tulsa in 1967. Ronnie's job sent him and his family all over the country. They had lived in Chicago, Florida, Virginia, Texas, and Ohio. I'd never had the opportunity to be the uncle that I had promised Dina and Kevin so many years before, and in that respect I felt cheated, I felt like I had failed them.

Spring arrived, it was early April 1990. Buck was visiting us in Tahlequah. We walked through the woods together and he enjoyed seeing the squirrels and jumping rabbits. We sat on a log and looked out at the scenic valley below. "Vince, I'm the luckiest boy in the whole world."

"You are? Why's that?"

"Because I've got two moms and two dads."

"Well, I'm pretty lucky myself. Because you're my son." We smiled at each other. He touched my hand, his little white hand seeming pale next to my dark skin. "Vince, how come you're brown and I'm white?"

I knew the day would come when he would ask that question, but it still caught me off guard. I thought a moment as he looked up at me.

"Well, ya see, son, God made us this way. He didn't want people to get bored. I mean, if everyone looked the same the world would be kind of yucky, don't ya think?" He nodded his head, "Like what, Vince?"

"If everybody was the same color and did the same things this old world wouldn't be half the fun it is now. What if you went to Japan and everyone was white? What if you went to Africa and everyone was white? Kinda dullsville, huh?"

"Yeah, Vince, like we wouldn't have pizza or Grandma's tortillas!"

"That's right. We'd all be sitting around looking at each other eating pork 'n' beans." He laughed when I said that, his question answered to his satisfaction. He stood and yelled, "Race you to the barn!" I lagged behind as my son ran with the wind across the pasture.

I came home from work one day and as I walked down the hallway Mica called out to me, "Hey, Dad look who's here." I stopped, then stepped into Mica's room. There sitting on Mica's bed was Sondra. Sondra and Mica had known each other since grade school when they were the power hitters on the Hoover Flames softball team. She was a pretty little girl, with a face full of freckles and a pretty smile. Her hair was black, blacker than black, and this did not surprise me. Sondra's mother was a beautician. For as long as I had known Sondra and her family, Sondra's hair had never been one color for more than six months at a time. I laughed out as I greeted her.

"Hi, Sondra! What happened to your hair?"

"Hi, Vince, do you like it?" she said beaming.

"I think I liked it better when it was green."

"Oh God, do you remember that?" she laughed.

"Pobrecita," I said, as I stepped closer to give her a hug, and she grinned and hugged me back. She was a nice girl, and I was glad Mica had a good friend. She stayed the weekend with us, then she returned to Tulsa. I saw her again a few months later, she was a platinum blonde.

May 1990 arrived. Debbie smiled as she talked on the phone to Becky DeGraw. Buck was signed up to play baseball. He was six years old and had tried out for the T-Ball League. His coach was astonished at his prowess. He watched in amazement as little Buck sent ball after ball into the outfield. The coach called out to his friend who coached the Coach Pitch League. The next thing Becky knew, Lance had been asked to play in the Coach Pitch League. He was now a member of the Owasso Cardinals.

I drove to Owasso after work for Buck's first baseball game. I wouldn't have missed this game for a million dollars. I thought of Dad. Together we had coached Buck, though not at the same time, and Buck had learned well. I stood by the chainlink fence near Buck's team bench, away from the other parents. I was as proud as any parent there. Buck played center field. I laughed as I watched him, he was hopping around holding himself as the first batter came to bat, he had to pee. It was a long three outs before Buck came running off the field yelling to me, "Where's the bathroom, Vince?" I pointed the way, and he was off at a dead run to the "Johnny on the spot."

He did well that game. The first two times at bat he grounded out, he was a little nervous, but his last two trips to the plate he hit a couple of doubles. In his fourth game Buck hit his first home run. It was a smash down the right-field line and rolled all the way to the fence. Buck was all smiles as his team surrounded him at home plate. I could feel Dad's presence, I knew that we shared the moment with our little slugger.

Sonny sat in the backseat as we drove to Buck's game. Buck sat beside me.

"Vince, will you be proud of me if we win?"

"Buck, I'd be proud of you if you lost."

His face beamed, "Thanks, Vince," he said, still smiling.

It was a happy summer that year watching Buck play ball. I remembered the baldheaded little boy who had endured chemotherapy. How brave my little boy was. I thanked God for bringing him into my life.

I drove to Mom's house one day after work. It was a Friday evening.

The phone rang, and I answered it. It was Debbie, and she was crying. She explained her dilemma, and in shock I hung up the phone. She had to have $3,800 by that evening or go to jail, the police had picked her up on bogus check charges. I grudgingly borrowed the money from Mom, then hurried to Tahlequah to keep Debbie from going to jail. Two weeks later Debbie closed the tamale plant and we returned to Tulsa.

In July 1990 Mom moved out of her home. She could not handle the memories that faced her every day in the now silent house. She had accepted the fact that Dad might die first, but she had thought she would always have Junior beside her. Now they were both gone. She was alone, and the once happy house was now a multiroom mausoleum. Dad and Junior came to her in dreams. She welcomed sleep and the brief reunions. But the dreams were not enough, the silence cried out through her. She would sit and cry with deep sobs, memory her only companion. The days grew longer, while the rooms grew smaller. For forty-nine years and eleven months she was wed. Now for the first time in her life she was alone. She wiped her eyes as her finger ran down the lines of apartments listed in the yellow pages. It was time to leave.

In August 1990 I qualified for the apprentice mechanic program sponsored by American Airlines. I was a stock clerk for American at its Tulsa base. The apprentice program had been ongoing for a few years now. The class I had qualified for would be the last. I saw it as a chance to better myself. Mechanics made good money, much more than a stock clerk. The only drawback was the seniority issue. I would lose my 1988 starting date. My starting date if I completed the course would be February 1991, three years down the tubes.

Over three hundred people from the American base at Tulsa had tested, and some had transferred from Chicago and other bases just for the opportunity. To prepare myself for the exam I bought one of the many "E-Z" mathematics books available. It had everything from addition to trigonometry in it. I thought of Dad and his correspondence course and how he had reached the same point in his life, now it was my turn to try and better myself for my wife and family.

Mica was enrolled at Tulsa Central, and Felicia had received a full athletic scholarship to play softball for Bacone College. The predominantly Indian school is located in Muskogee, Oklahoma. Mother's cousin Alec McIntosh, better known as Acee Blue Eagle, had graduated from Bacone and taught art there, the first of many Indian artists. His works are known around the world, Russia, Europe, Ethiopia. He painted a mural on the U.S.S. *Oklahoma*, which now lies silent at the bottom of Pearl Harbor. Acee is buried on the grounds of the Thomas Gilcrease Museum in Tulsa.

Test day arrived, and I faced it with nervous anticipation. The exam room was filled with men and women. I was glad to see the women in the room. As the father of two girls I was glad that women would have the same opportunity to succeed as men. A tall Indian girl smiled when she saw me. I returned her smile, the look was there, the proud acknowledgment of our heritage.

Two weeks passed before the results of the test were posted on the company bulletin board in the main office. They would take only the top forty individuals. The remainder would continue at their jobs. I walked over to the facility on my lunch break. I scanned the list of names, which were not in any order. The print seemed too small. I didn't see my name, so I checked again, this time more slowly. A smile crossed my face, I took a deep breath, I saw my name on the list of those accepted into the program. We would have class four nights a week, from five to ten o'clock, at a vo-tech facility near the airport. I sat with two other stock clerks as the rest of the future mechanics entered the room. One of them was the tall Indian girl that I had seen in the exam room.

For five months I studied. Every waking moment I spent with my head in a book. I had never studied so hard in all my life, but at the end of my rainbow I knew that there was indeed a pot of gold.

On Christmas morning we welcomed Becky, Sonny, and Lance to our small apartment. Felicia was home from college and we were happy that once again we were all together. Felicia and Mica played with Buck. They enjoyed listening to him ask questions. They teased and joked, and laughter filled the room.

In January 1991 our entire class graduated from the course. We all went to a nearby bar to celebrate. I didn't drink, but this was a special occasion. I was surprised at the cost of the beer. My last beer had cost a quarter.

Our class began on-the-job training with the American Airlines mechanics in February. I was assigned to hangar 3, on the 727 line. I was impressed by the dedication of these men. Though markedly different in appearance, some grubby looking while others were neat and clean, they were all professionals, proud of their craft, and well they should be. In their hands were the lives of millions. I developed a deep respect for these men in blue, who wore the red and blue letter "A" proudly on their shirts. They are unsung heroes who strive daily for perfection, for anything less is unacceptable.

In March 1991 we received heartbreaking news. Bucky's cancer had returned. He began chemotherapy immediately. The cancer was in all parts of his body, he limped because of the pain in his leg and hip. He accepted his illness bravely. He told Becky one day as they drove home from the hospital, "Mama, if they have to cut off my leg will you get me a little wheelchair? I don't think I can handle a big one." I wished I could trade places with him.

I visited him in the hospital when he took his chemotherapy. A friend of Becky and Sonny's was there and Buck introduced me as his best friend. That really touched my heart. I silently cursed God for doing this to my son. As I was about to leave, a little tear ran down his cheek and he wailed my name, "Vince."

"What is it, son?"

"I'm losing my hair, Vince," he started to cry. He was seven and a half years old, it was hard for him to see his hair fall out. I quickly tried to cheer him.

"Hey, summertime is coming. Baseball starts next month, you'll be cool with that hair gone, and everyone is wearing their hair cut to the scalp anyway. You'll fit right in!"

"Ya think so, Vince?"

"Sure, son."

He smiled and looked at Becky as he wiped the tears from his eyes. I kissed him and he smiled as I waved goodbye from the doorway.

It was a rainy Sunday afternoon. Debbie answered the knock at the door. It was Becky and Buck. He smiled as he limped to me. I hugged him and kissed him, and he smiled and wrapped his arms around me. He walked back to Becky and brought me a small gift. It was a pocketknife. I thanked him and hugged him for it and he beamed with pride at having pleased me. I thought a moment about the knife that I had for Buck. It was a big survival knife with a compass on the end, and inside the handle were fishhooks and line. I had shown it to him several times and he'd looked at it with awe. I told him he could have it when he joined the Boy Scouts and he agreed to wait. Now I stood and walked to the hall closet. I pulled the knife in its sheath from the darkness and handed it to Buck. His eyes danced as he held his precious gift. I cautioned him not ever to run with it and not to use it until he and I went into the woods together. He promised that he wouldn't. We sat and talked. He liked M. C. Hammer, the music sent his little shoulders twitching as he kept time to the rhythm. A 1–900 commercial came on the television and Buck smiled at the pretty girls.

"Hey, Vince, I'm going to call those girls and tell them I'm thirty years old."

I looked at him in surprise and he giggled at the expression on my face. All too soon our visit ended and my son and his mother drove home to Owasso.

April arrived, and Debbie and I were having trouble again. She was acting strange. I had given her $500 to give to our attorney. Three weeks
later when I called him he said he hadn't seen her in months; he didn't
have the $500. She blew up when I asked her about the money, she had no
explanation. We were fighting over little things now, the mailbox key for
one. She said she only had one key. When I talked to the apartment manager she said she had given Debbie two keys. The final straw was when
Debbie called out another man's name in her sleep. It happened more than
once. Then she admitted her affair. That was it. I thought of the kids. Felicia was in college, Mica would graduate from high school next year. It
was time for me to do what I should have done years ago. The kids were
old enough to understand. I loved Deb, but I couldn't live with her. We
went to an inexpensive divorce company in Tulsa. Mica would stay with
Debbie, I would pay child support. We had the paperwork started.

I moved back into the house on West Brady. I stood in the living room
and looked at the dining room. The house that had been my dream come
true as a nine-year-old was now my sanctuary. I remembered the many
Christmas gatherings we'd had there. The memories of my life raced
through my mind. I walked to my bedroom door. Gone were the pictures
of Sandra Dee that I had pinned on the wall, and the picture of Johnny
Unitas, arm cocked, ready to throw another touchdown pass. I looked at
the bedroom window. Every night as a teenager I would look out that window at the moon and wonder what my future would be. What would I be?
Where would I travel? I thought of Dad and Junior. I wished Dad was
there. I needed to talk to him. He didn't want me to marry Debbie, maybe
that was why I did. He called her a party girl. While I was in the Marines
Debbie continued going to the Mexican dances and of course, being
young and beautiful, she attracted a lot of attention. Dad didn't want me
dating her when I came back. He had really liked Bonnie until her father
ruined everything. Dad in his infinite wisdom had been right all along.
And I, as always, had been wrong. I walked through the empty house to
the kitchen. What a happy place Mama's kichen had always been. Suddenly I felt a presence, I knew that it must be Dad and Junior. I was no
longer lonely.

One evening I stopped in to see Mica. She met me at the door, she
wanted to talk to me. She told me that she wanted to live with me. Debbie
had told her that she was going to ask for $400 a month in child support so
that she could redecorate the apartment. Mica knew that Debbie would

not spend the money for her school clothes. Mica did not want to be used. The next week she moved in with me.

When Debbie and I returned to the divorce counselor she informed Debbie that she would have to pay child support, since Mica was living with me. I asked for $100 a month. The counselor advised more, but I settled on that amount.

During the months of March and April I had noticed that Debbie's right breast had changed. The nipple had become coarse, but I could not get her to see a doctor. Once we were separated I dismissed the thought from my mind.

May arrived. Mica and I stopped in to see Debbie one afternoon. The phone rang, Debbie's face went pale as she talked on the phone. Buck had collapsed, he was in the hospital. We were at the hospital often as Buck fought for his life. Two weeks passed and still no progress. The doctors could do no more for my son. We were allowed to visit him one last time. I was told that he could hear but could not respond because of the medication. I entered his room quietly. He lay on a bed wearing a large diaper. His face was swollen, tubes entered his little body. I spoke loudly so that he could hear.

"Hey, Buck, it's me, Vince. Hey, hurry and get well so we can play some ball, okay? I love you, son. Of course you know that, don't you, big guy? Mica and Felicia are fine, and that darn Heidi is still snoring all night."

I didn't want him to hear me cry, I had to concentrate in order to keep from breaking down. "When you get well, you and me are going to the woods, okay? I've gotta go now, son. I love you."

On 15 May 1991 Buck passed away. I cried to the heavens when I got the news. My little baby boy was gone, I knew that I would mourn his passing until my dying day.

I stood looking down at Bucky as he lay in his casket. Debbie wept beside me. He wore a green shirt and his black M. C. Hammer pants. He looked as if he were asleep. He was still the good-looking boy he had always been. His funeral service was held in Tulsa. Sonny and Becky bought three plots, Buck's was in the middle. I was a pallbearer. After the service, the other pallbearers and I waited for the funeral home directors to move the little white casket out to the hearse. I saw the minister standing alone. I walked over and told him of Lance's visitor in the hospital and his earlier miraculous recovery. I also told him how Lance had wept and wanted to see his friend again. Now he was with his friend, the realization brought me peace of mind.

We stood at the gravesite as the minister repeated Lance's story. Afterward the pallbearers placed their boutonnieres on the casket, I was the last one to do so. As I stepped back from the casket the flowers that I had put there fell to the ground. Before I could stoop to pick it up, the boutonniere flipped into the open grave. I knew Lance was there. I smiled. "I love you too, son," I said softly. He was part of the invisible world now, the flower flipping into his grave reinforced my belief in my great-grandfather's teachings. Our spirits would meet again.

Lance's little teammates were there with helium-filled balloons. As Sonny and Becky walked away from the grave the little boys yelled, "Good-bye, Lance," releasing their balloons. As the balloons rose to the cloud-filled sky, Becky DeGraw collapsed to the ground in tears.

During the weeks following Lance's death I cried daily. Usually it was while driving to and from work. I was forty-three years old and afraid of no man, yet the loss of my son reduced me to jelly. My little boy had saved my life when I was in despair, now he was gone. I felt so alone without him.

As I worked on the landing gear of the 727 my mind was on Debbie. I had to get her to our doctor. I had to know if she was all right, it gnawed at my insides. I called our family doctor and told the secretary that I was bringing her in after work with or without an appointment. We sat in the exam room. Debbie was cheerful. She was too cheerful, I knew she was disguising her fear. I sat silently as Doctor Childers entered the room. He examined Debbie and then made her an appointment for a mammogram the next day. We returned two days later for the mammogram test results. Once again we sat in the little exam room. Debbie was noticeably nervous. Doctor Childers entered the room with a solemn look on his face.

"I'm afraid I have bad news for you, Debbie."

Her eyes began to water as the doctor continued. "You have breast cancer, Debbie. I'm so sorry." He hugged her and she sniffled on his shoulder as I sat in shock. He had been our family doctor for over twenty years, now all he could do was hold her. His eyes watered and his voice was shaky with emotion.

"We're going to run some tests. I'll call you later when we have everything set up." We walked out of his office arm in arm.

I couldn't leave her . . . not now. I remembered our wedding vows, "through sickness and health," over and over, the words driving home the love I had for her. She had treated me like dirt over the years and yet I was still crazy about her, maybe I was just crazy period. What is it that makes a person behave this way? I should have left her years ago, yet now I couldn't leave her to die alone. This one-sided love was insane, but who said the world was sane?

She moved out of the apartment and into the house on West Brady at the end of May. Sonny and Becky helped us. They looked odd without Lance, I was so used to seeing the three of them. We laughed and joked as we went about the task of moving. They were good people, it felt good having friends like them.

Debbie and I never returned to the divorce counselor. The dreaded cancer had brought the reality of life crashing down upon us. We clung to each other as never before.

On 1 June 1991 Debbie had a breast biopsy. On 5 June she complained of back pain. X-rays found nothing so Doctor Childers ordered a CAT scan. Cancer was found in her ninth rib. It was inoperable because it was so close to the spine. On 8 June they performed a back biopsy on her ninth rib, but there was not enough rib left to get a thorough exam; they performed a suction biopsy on her later. On 20 June they installed a port for future chemotherapy. On 25 June we received the diagnosis. Debbie had inflammatory carcinoma, a rare form of cancer that travels through the blood stream, through the veins from one point to another. The cancer had traveled from her breast to her ninth rib.

On 1 July 1991 Debbie began cobalt radiation. On 22 July 1991 she started chemotherapy. She began with enthusiasm, determined to whip cancer. She had me shave her head. She would not lose her hair to cancer, she would take her own hair. She had courage. I was proud that she handled herself so well. I don't know how I would have held up if she had been whiny and had given up. The chemo took its toll on her. Her treatments were on Monday, and she would feel nauseated through Thursday. Friday through Sunday she was fine, but she always cried on Sunday because she knew that the cycle would begin again on Monday.

Chemotherapy kills cancer cells all right, but it kills healthy cells too. In time it can kill you. It shuts down organs and brings on pneumonia.

Debbie lay on the couch nauseated, I sat on the floor beside her, nearby was a large paper sack with a plastic trash liner inside. I would wipe her mouth with a washcloth after she threw up. Felicia and Mica would care for her when I went to work on the evening shift.

The managers and supervisors at American Airlines gave me a special privilege. Normally, mechanics rotate shifts, days, evenings, midnights. I was given the okay to remain on evening shift so that I could take Debbie in for her chemotherapy during the week. The people at American were super, they were like a big family. They helped tremendously in our time of need.

By August the oncologist gave Debbie no hope of surviving. He said she would remain on chemo until she passed away, some time within fourteen months. This infuriated Debbie, she would not give up, she would never give up. She told the doctor that she would not roll over and die. She would seek other avenues. This made the doctor angry, he slammed the door as he stormed from the room. I think what made him mad was the fact that my insurance company would not be sending him the $2,600 per week that was his fee.

It was mid-October when Debbie tried to call her sister in Largo, Florida. She hit a wrong digit and by chance contacted a large cancer research center in Florida. She thought it was fate that this had occurred. She spoke with the director of the center, and in November she flew to Tampa to be examined.

Doctor Childers conferred with the center in Florida. Meanwhile, a mastectomy was scheduled for mid-November. We walked into the hospital room at six in the morning. Debbie began to get undressed as the nurse told her about the procedures. There was a knock at the door, and Becky DeGraw entered. She talked with us for a while, encouraging Debbie, then she turned to me. "Look what I've got," she said and opened a locket that hung around her neck. It was a picture of Buck. Before I could control myself tears rushed from my eyes. It happened so fast, as if by reflex. I turned away from Becky. She apologized and patted my back. It was over as fast as it had begun. I cleared my throat and admired the cute picture of my son.

After surgery Debbie was in quite a bit of pain. All I could do was place ice on her lips so she could get some liquid into her. Her sisters visited her, they cried as they watched her. The next day she was moved into a private room. She was feeling better, she asked for her makeup. A few days later we returned home. Sitting quietly on the edge of the bed, she looked at me and her eyes filled with tears.

"Oh, Vincent, I've been so rotten to you." She began to cry. "How can you love me? Can we forget the past? Please? Let's start over, okay?" She laid her head on my chest and cried like a baby. I held her until her crying ceased.

But soon she became depressed, she was quiet, that wasn't like her. One evening I sat down beside her on our bed and held her hand as she looked at her bandaged chest. "I want to tell you something," I said. "The loss of your breast in no way changes my love or desire for you. It doesn't bother me, so don't let it bother you. I know you feel awkward, but you're alive. I love you, not your breast or your limbs. Remember our wedding vows? For richer and for poorer, through sickness and health. Well, we've definitely lived the poor life and you're really sick, but I love you, I always will." Tears welled in her eyes as she laid her head on my shoulder. "I love you," she said. Two weeks later we made love. Her depression vanished.

By the time December arrived she was a bundle of energy. She was happy, she appreciated life. We walked hand in hand now. What a shame it was to waste all those years. It took this dreaded disease to bring us together, to make her realize that I had always been there for her. We walked through Utica Square, window shopping. The people from American Airlines had donated $1,000 to us for Christmas. Debbie bought everything she could for the girls. She laid her head on my shoulder, "I want to be just like Joe and Virginia Rodrigues, so in love, and always together." We stopped at Santa's House. I missed Buck. We watched in silence as children entered Santa's House. We remembered the times we'd shared there with Buck. We kissed, as the children giggled and pointed at us.

In February 1992 Debbie began radiation treatments. She received thirty-eight treatments on her chest and lymph nodes. Everyone at the treatment center liked Debbie. She was a bundle of energy and all smiles as she greeted everyone she saw. She brought courage and hope to the other patients. I was proud of my Debbie. She had grit, her strength made it easier for me. This entire episode seemed like a horrible dream to me. Each morning I hoped that I would awake and this nightmare would be over. This can't be real, my subconscious would echo to me, this can't be happening to my Debbie. Over and over I would think this thought as we entered the hospital week after week.

In March 1992 Felicia told us she was pregnant. We were heartbroken.

We would keep the child, father or not. What else could happen? After the initial shock of the news, Debbie became excited. She hoped and prayed that she would live long enough to hold her grandchild. Myself, I concentrated on helping Debbie, she was my main concern.

In April 1992 Debbie flew to Tampa, Florida, to be tested for a possible bone marrow transplant. She returned to Tulsa happy. She would be able to have the transplant as soon as a bed was available. One week later the phone rang, her room was ready. We flew to Tampa, Debbie's sister and husband picked us up at the airport. We stayed with them a day, then the time came for Debbie to check into her room. We stopped outside the entrance to the hospital. She looked up at the blue sky and white clouds. She took a deep breath, then we went in. When we entered the sterile room, the nurse asked me to step outside. I stood just outside the doorway. I could see clearly through the glass wall. Debbie began to strip and as she did she began to cry. I felt a heavy hand on my shoulder. I thought it was my brother-in-law, but no one was there when I turned around. Maybe it was Dad, or Oscar. I flew back to Tulsa the next day. Debbie would not begin her bone marrow transplant for several days.

During the month of April I began dropping tools. My hands would go to sleep, my back would cramp, and I was short of breath after climbing only one flight of stairs. Something was wrong, but I shrugged it off. I was working in the door shop now, the month before I had been working on the tail section of an MD-80. I walked up and down stairs all day long, suddenly now I was gasping for breath. Later I learned that I had developed asthma and bronchitis.

Unknown to me, my co-workers were donating their vacation days on my behalf so that I could be with Debbie. Most of the days came from my apprentice mechanic class, the rest came from volunteers in other shops and hangars. The person who spearheaded the drive was June Sewell, to her and my co-workers I will be eternally grateful. My supervisor notified me that I had forty-four days of vacation donated.

On 8 May 1992 Debbie had her bone marrow transplant. She was doing well and might possibly be discharged by month's end. On 22 May I drove to Tampa. I found an apartment in a complex close to the hospital, set up for the cancer patients and their families. Everything needed for everyday living was provided: linens, silverware, coffeemakers, television, furniture, refrigerator.

Debbie was discharged on 30 May 1992 but required to live within five minutes of the hospital. Twenty-four-hour care was needed for the discharged patient. I was taught how to draw blood from the Hickman catheter, also how to flush the lines with saline solution and heparin. I was also taught how to change her dressing. Her first week out of the hospital I would take blood samples daily to the bone marrow clinic. After that I was required to take blood twice a week for the duration of our stay.

We joined the "Umbrella Gang," the name I had given them when I first noticed the gathering of masked and unmasked people who sat by the swimming pool in the cool of the evening. They were patients (they had to wear something like a surgeon's mask to reduce the risk of infection) and their relatives. They came from all over the United States, and one couple was from England. I sat one evening talking to an older gentleman named Ed. He had lost his wife to cancer and now his daughter had it. He told me that when his wife was in the hospital the divorce lawyers were thick as fleas. Men were divorcing their wives because they were ill. I couldn't believe it, what a bunch of sorry bastards they were.

The comradeship of the Umbrella Gang was much needed. We became like family, all concerned with one another's well-being. It was group therapy at its best. You would think we were doctors the way we sat around discussing white blood counts, and platelets, or who got blood today, who had fever or diarrhea. We knew each other's conditions because we cared.

Two weeks after Debbie's discharge her arm became swollen. I rushed her to the hospital. When they admitted her she began to cry, not from pain but from the hatred of hospitals. She wanted to be with me and the gang. She spent another week in the hospital.

We spent the Fourth of July with Stella and Earl, Debbie's sister and brother-in-law. We were watching fireworks in the neighborhood. While Debbie, Stella, and I were looking in one direction Earl was looking elsewhere. Suddenly he yelled, "Boy, look at that big white one there."

We turned around but saw nothing. Earl was still oohing.

Then Stella said, "Put your glasses on, McGoo, that's a street light!" We had a good laugh.

The next evening we sat with our friends near the pool. Debbie let everyone know that we would soon be grandparents, everyone was excited for us. The couple from England, Ken and Bridget, presented me with two sketches that Ken had drawn of the Umbrella Gang. One picture shows the crowded gathering in the evening, the other suggests that someday with God's will there will no longer be a need for the Umbrella Gang, the empty chairs symbolizing the victory over cancer.

On 14 July 1992 we said goodbye to our dear friends at the apartment complex. We especially thanked Henryetta, the apartment manager. She was a wonderful person, so giving, so thoughtful of others.

Debbie was happy as we pulled out onto the interstate. She marveled at everything. The fear of death wakens the awareness in each of us. I had felt the same way when I went to Vietnam. As we drove toward Georgia she smiled, "This past year, even though I've been sick, has been the happiest year of my life."

"It has?"

"I never knew how much you loved me."

"I've always loved you."

She scooted across the seat and kissed me. We drove the rest of the trip side by side. We spent the night just outside Atlanta. The next morning, with Debbie as my navigator, we took a wrong turn and got lost in the maze of Atlanta highways. As I cussed the morning traffic, she laughed heartily, "You'll never change, will you?" Then I got tickled and we laughed together.

As we entered Tennessee she spoke of visiting the birthplace of Alvin York. *Sergeant York* was her favorite movie. She especially liked the part where Alvin York gave up his evil ways and gave himself to the Lord. She identified with that. We stopped at a tourism center and found that the birthplace would be too far out of the way for us to visit.

We did stop and visit Bettye Jones, a good friend of ours whose daughter Terri had lived across the street from us in Tulsa. Terri was a delightful woman in her early thirties. She had no children, and she loved the company of Mica and Felicia. A graduate of Purdue University, Terri was active with the radio and television women of Tulsa. As busy as she was, she always found time to take Felicia and Mica roller skating on the river parks, or to a movie. They spent a lot of time together just talking. Every summer Bob and Bettye would visit Terri. They were a handsome couple, and our family liked them from the moment we met. Bob was an executive, he loved to play golf. Being a golfer myself, I hit it off with him immediately. He had an air of confidence about him and yet I could tell he was a sincere and kind person, as was his striking wife Bettye. She had slightly graying hair and was pretty. Terri favored her. Bettye enjoyed gardening, as did Terri. Debbie and I enjoyed their company.

Terri was slain in her backyard by a jealous boyfriend. Bob and Bettye were heartbroken, as were the rest of us. Weeks after the funeral I would see Felicia sitting on the porch looking across the street at the vacant brick house. Tears would fill her eyes as she sat thinking of her friend Terri. She would forever ask, why? Felicia would name her first child Terri, that way Terri would always be with her. Bettye lost Bob to cancer a few years after Terri's death. But Bettye, being the strong and intelligent woman that she is, has gone on with her life, and I know that Bob and Terri are with her. We visited Bettye for two days, then we drove home to Tulsa.

Teresa Marie Porter was born 28 July 1992 in Tulsa, Oklahoma. We were now grandparents. I marveled at the newborn with the full head of black hair. Her father was Indian, Seminole, Cherokee, and Choctaw. Our granddaughter Terri was a mixture of proud blood. Debbie and I were on cloud nine as we looked at the pretty little girl. Debbie thanked God for letting her live long enough for this moment. Together we stood with our arms around each other as we looked at our first grandchild through the hospital's nursery window.

"I can't believe that I'm a grandma," Debbie said softly. "Isn't she precious?"

Debbie returned to Florida for a checkup on 3 August. When she returned she gave us the good news, she was cancer-free. Our prayers had been answered. Debbie felt wonderful. We babysat for Felicia, and at times I would just watch my Debbie hold our granddaughter, witnessing the love in her eyes as she kissed the baby over and over.

In September I was tested and found to have carpal tunnel syndrome. The doctor wanted to operate right away, but I wanted a second opinion. I saw two other doctors and they each confirmed the diagnosis. I decided to delay surgery. I had to take care of Debbie. She still tired easily, her body had yet to regain its strength from the ravages of the bone marrow transplant. She needed me, and I would not let her down.

November arrived, and Debbie, Linda, and I flew to Tampa for Debbie's checkup. The day after her test we entered the small hospital room to hear about the results. The doctor was straightforward with us. "Debbie, we have found cancer lesions on your liver. There is no cure for liver cancer. You have at the most six months to live." The doctor's female assistant sniffled.

"Do I have any options?" Debbie asked.

"You can go home and enjoy the quality time that you have left, or you can try chemotherapy again, which will cause sickness. The last two weeks of your life you will go into a coma, then you will die."

We returned to Tulsa. "I wish we could have lived on a farm together again," Debbie said. "I loved my little chickens." We sat in the living room, Debbie held little Terri and kissed her. She laid the baby down on the sofa and stood looking at her, "I wish I could be there for her when she grows up," then she began to cry. "Oh, Vincent, I just want to be normal!" She turned and grabbed me. She cried deep sobs against my chest. All I could do was hold her tight.

Christmas was a happy occasion. We spent the day at Linda's house, as we had for the past two years. We listened to Mexican music and danced. Ronnie and Debbie had fun dancing with each other, and of course everyone pigged out on Mom's tamales.

On New Year's Eve Debbie and I went to the Creek Nation Bingo Hall in Tulsa. Debbie loved her bingo, she loved Las Vegas, and the track too. I guess her entire life had been a gamble. As midnight struck she began to cry, "Oh, Vincent, this is my last New Year's Eve party." She grabbed me and we kissed liked young lovers.

In January she started chemotherapy. We talked during her treatments. She wanted me to remarry, she wanted someone to take care of me, she didn't want me to be alone. And I would always counter her suggestion with, "Look, I can take care of myself. I was a sergeant in the Marine Corps, remember?" She would say, "Yes, but you were in the post office," then we would laugh. She took my hand and looked into my eyes, "I want you to be happy. You deserve to be happy. I love you so."

In March she was examined again. The chemotherapy had done nothing to the cancer. Her entire liver was covered with lesions. She wanted to go to Las Vegas one last time. So Debbie, Mom, and I flew to Las Vegas. I felt so sorry for her. She couldn't win a thing. Mom and I were winning money left and right. I would give Debbie my slot machine and it would quit paying out. I gave her rack after rack of my hundred dollars' worth of coins and she would lose. I felt awful for her. Watching her play blackjack, I suddenly saw her grimace and hold her side. My heart sank. We went back to our room and returned home the next day.

April arrived. In a last-ditch effort to survive, Debbie tried a new drug called Taxol. The drug poisoned her system. Blisters broke out in her mouth, in her groin area, and inside her. I stayed with her, taking care of her. I emptied her bedpan and swabbed her blistered groin with ointment. I did everything I could to comfort her. She told me she was not in pain at all. She didn't need morphine. Though it caused her discomfort to talk, she would squeeze my hand and say, "I love you so much," and I would kiss her hand.

The head nurse called me outside. "Mr. Mendoza, your wife is dying, there's nothing that can be done. You need to go ahead and make arrangements, she won't last too much longer."

"Oh no, you're mistaken, she'll bounce back, you wait and see. You don't know my Debbie."

The nurse looked into my eyes, "I'm so sorry," she said, and turned and walked away. When Debbie fell asleep I left the hospital and drove to the cemetery. I bought two plots just behind Lance's grave.

Easter arrived. Spring was Debbie's favorite time of year. I held her hand as she breathed deeply. The room was filled with family and friends. Felicia and Mica wept next to her. I watched her eyes as she breathed her last deep raspy breath. I saw the glimmer of life leave my Debbie. I remembered the beautiful girl at the Mexican dance so many years ago. Now her eyes stared blankly in death. She had left me behind and I wanted to be with her. I left the room after the others. I walked like a zombie, still dazed at Debbie's death. I walked to the desk and called the funeral home in Sand Springs. They would send someone. I waited in another room with Sonny DeGraw. Then I returned to Debbie's side. The tubes had been removed. I stood and looked at her still body. Then it hit me and I cried out, "Oh, my poor baby!" I kissed her, then laid my head on her chest and cried.

Sonny drove me home. The girls were already there. Debbie had died just before eight o'clock that evening. Now it was eleven. The girls were in bed, and I sat and cried in the living room. Suddenly I felt a peacefulness come over me. It flowed from the top of my head to the bottoms of my feet, filling me completely with a calm. Somehow I knew that Debbie was at peace, I couldn't cry anymore. At midnight Mica came into the living room, "Daddy, I felt Mama rubbing my feet, like she used to do when I was little."

"She's letting you know that she's all right, and not to mourn her."

Just then Felicia entered the room, "Daddy, I felt somebody rubbing my feet and when I looked no one was there."

"It was Mama," Mica said, and they looked at each other in silence.

The funeral was held in Sand Springs. Faith Bible Church, the little church that Debbie and I came to love was not large enough to hold a great number of people. Reverend Gus Talburt officiated at the service. We loved to hear him preach, the music that was played for the Lord at the little church was energetic and full of love. At my request my friend Bobby played three songs at the funeral: ''Vaya Con Dios,'' ''The Dance,'' and ''I Will Always Love You.''

Debbie is buried in Tulsa, a few feet away from Lance. My plot is next to Debbie's. My friend Wayne lies three hundred yards to the west.

I returned to work the next week. I had never felt so alone in my life. Felicia and her baby moved out months before, and Mica had moved to Oklahoma City after graduation. The shop where I worked had been Debbie's shop too. She had been the secretary. Everyone knew her and expressed their condolences. When it was time for the morning break everyone settled down to eat doughnuts and drink coffee. I hurried to the phone as always. Halfway there I stopped, there was no one to call. Debbie was gone. Loneliness embraced me. I slowly walked to the break room to join the other mechanics.

After work I drove to Sand Springs to eat at our favorite restaurant. I ordered my usual meal and sat at a booth facing the entrance. I watched as elderly people entered arm in arm with their lifelong partners. I felt cheated and angry. Debbie and I had talked in Florida about growing old together, the two of us sitting on the porch waiting for our grandchildren to visit. She could hardly wait for me to get a gray hair. My dream of growing old with the one I loved had been snuffed out. As I looked at the gray-haired couples I felt sad. Soon one of them would be left alone in the world. They too would hear the deafening silence of their home.

The phone rang, I slowly walked to answer it and sat in Debbie's antique chair. It was Felicia and Debbie's friend Alice Gwin. I had met her twice, she was attractive, and about our age. She and Felicia had worked together at a tax company in Tulsa. She had helped us with our taxes in the fall of 1992 and February 1993. She wanted to speak to Felicia, I told her that if I saw Felicia I would tell her that she had called.

May arrived and I called my Mexican buddies. The Kentucky Derby would be run on Saturday, and Eddie, Tommy, and Meatball were raring to go. I picked them up at Eddie's house early Saturday morning and we drove to Blue Ribbon Downs, where the Derby would be shown on simulcast. As we drove, the sound of folding paper could be heard as each friend checked and double-checked his racing form. Meatball smiled at me and said, "I never will forget the morning Debbie came by the house and picked up Pam. Debbie had $500, they went to the track that day." He saw the look of surprise on my face, and he began to laugh.

"Didn't she tell you about it?"

"Hell, no!"

Everyone laughed as I shook my head. We arrived at the track and soon had placed our bets. We had every horse covered except one, no way could it win. I sat at a table near the entrance with my friends. I was drinking beer with them, why not? I looked at the crowd of people, hoping that I would see my Debbie walking toward me. I remembered our last trip to this track. She had packed a picnic basket with cheese, crackers, and wine. We had won big on the last three races, she was happy. I looked about at the crowd of people. I felt close to Debbie just being there. That was truly the reason I had come at all.

The trance was broken as Eddie in his gravelly voice said, "Man, Vince, we're going to win this time. I've got a feeling, y'know. We got 'em all covered except that nag Sea Hero. Yep, we're going to go home winners today, Bud."

The excitement mounted as Derby time neared. Soon the elite field of horses entered the starting gate. They were off, and a cheer rang out from the crowd. The winning horse crossed the finish line, we tore our tickets in two and threw them in the air. "That nag Sea Hero" had won! Then we, the Wile E. Coyotes of the race track, stomped back to my car and drove home. There would be another race, and another day.

I sat at my large oak desk looking at the stack of medical bills piled high. I had been paying what I could every payday for what seemed like forever. Still the bills arrived, new ones mixed with the old. Health care facilities, radiologist, internist, oncologist, anesthesiologist, hospitals, not to mention the rent, utilities, car insurance, groceries. I handled them well, satisfying each wolf as it came to my door. If I could only hold out until the life insurance money arrived I would be fine.

I had chosen only the minimum of life insurance offered by my employer because Debbie and I had always been healthy, neither of us dreamed that anything devastating would happen.

Alice called one June day just to see how I was doing. We talked for quite a while. Felicia had helped her move back to her little house in Crowder, Oklahoma, near the edge of Lake Eufaula. Her ex-husband had died, leaving her the house they had shared in joint tenancy. I found her to be an intelligent and very sincere person.

The life insurance money arrived in the nick of time. I sat relieved. The bills would be paid off. As I placed the stamp on the last bill I happened to look toward the hallway. I saw Debbie step out of the dining room and walk toward Felicia's room. She wore the yellow nightgown that her sister had made for her. I smiled as I watched her enter Felicia's room. I stood and slowly followed. I knew she would be gone when I got there. The room was empty.

"I love you, baby." I said softly, then turned and walked back to my desk.

I called Alice one evening just to chat, and she invited me down to her place to go fishing. I remembered her drawing the map for Debbie. We had planned to visit her just before Debbie became ill for the last time. As I pulled in front of the small house near a sprawling catalpa tree I was eager to visit with Alice face to face. She fixed coffee and we sat at the kitchen table talking. The more we talked the more I liked her. She despised gambling, she couldn't see wasting good hard-earned money. She was in the process of starting her own tax business, she had clients in the area. She showed me her twenty-two acres, and I looked at the neglected property, thinking to myself how I would hate to be the unlucky soul that had to clean up this mess. The weeds were high, the trees needed trimming back, a large fallen shed whose beams had been splintered by a tornado lay like bones in the waist-deep grass. It began to rain, dashing my hopes of fishing. We visited the rest of the afternoon. I took her out to dinner, at her suggestion we drove to Krebs, Oklahoma, home of the best Italian cooking I had ever tasted. I was impressed. I drove home glad that I had made a new friend.

In June I drove to the Claremore Indian Hospital in Claremore, Oklahoma. As I entered, I was amazed at the number of white faces that were there. Very few had dominant Indian features. In fact if these people had been standing in a crowd, I couldn't have picked out the ones who had Indian blood. The facility had been remodeled, everything appeared neat and clean. I walked to the register area and provided the clerk with my certificate of degree of Indian blood. I was then directed to the surgery clinic's appointment desk, where I signed in, then returned to the hallway. The surgery clinic was a few feet from pediatrics, sick children passed by sneezing and coughing nonstop for the next five hours as I sat waiting. Finally my name was called and I met the with a doctor who would get the process started. He would order the medical reports from the other doctors that I had seen. My surgery was scheduled for mid-August. I filed a worker's compensation claim, then notified American Airlines of my intent.

By August, Alice and I had agreed that I should move in with her. She was a wonderful person. She was my best friend. We shared the same values and dreams. I can't say enough about her. Mom had sold her house in April, and the new owner had notified me that he had resold the property and that I needed to be out by the end of August. Alice's marriage had not gone well, and Debbie's death made me realize that life is too short to spend it being miserable. Together we talked of what we desired and expected in a relationship. Neither of us would tolerate lies, greed, or unfaithfulness. It was our second chance at happiness. I had sacrificed for the sake of my children, it had been well worth it, but now I was free. No more heartache, only happiness. As we unloaded the last of my belongings off my truck a rooster crowed. I thought of Grandma's camp house and I smiled.

On 23 August I had my surgery. I was told that it would take less than forty-five minutes. Hours later I was wheeled out of the operating room. I had nothing but trouble from the start. The normal healing time for this wrist surgery is four to six weeks. October arrived and I was still in pain. By mid-November I was feeling better. I obtained a release from the hospital and returned to work. American Airlines gave me the easiest job in my new shop. I worked four days, then my hand became swollen and the pain began again. The next day I reported to the Indian hospital.

As I walked around the corner near the surgery clinic, an old Indian woman spoke to me from her wheelchair. She looked to be in her eighties. "What are you doing here?" she asked.

I stopped and smiled at her, "Sometimes I wonder, Grandmother."

"I've been sitting here for two hours, and you're the first Indian I've seen come around that corner."

"I know, Grandmother, I know."

"You'd think that you would at least have to look like an Indian to be here. Not blond-haired with blue eyes, or red-headed. It's pitiful," she said as she shook her head.

The doctor recommended more therapy. I returned home. The next

Wednesday, 24 November 1993, I was laid off with a number of other aircraft mechanics.

December arrived, and I stood in line to receive Indian commodities. I looked around the unheated room at the needy people. I never would have believed that I would be here among them. All my working life I had given to the United Way, now I needed help. I received commodities until March.

On 4 April 1994 Alice and I were married in Fort Smith, Arkansas. Alice was a godsend. When Debbie passed away I knew that I didn't want to get involved with a woman my age who had grown children. Her children might be unhappy, thinking that I would infringe on their inheritance. I didn't want to marry a young woman either, I didn't want to raise a wife, and I sure didn't want to marry a woman with little children. I was set in my mind that I would be alone, but I would have my children and Terri. The spirits that watched over me must have brought me Alice, she had no children. We were compatible from the beginning.

In May I decided to enter the North American Indian Prose Award competition. Alice and I went to see a Cherokee medicine man who lived near Tahlequah. We waited in the driveway, three other cars were there. Two were occupied. We would wait our turn to see the chosen one. It was a clear day, cattle grazed in the pasture on either side of the house. The door to the house opened and an Indian lady emerged. She walked quickly down the gravel drive to her car. The medicine man stood clearly in the doorway, Alice had never seen a medicine man and she looked intently at the tall, striking figure. He held a pan of water. As we watched, he stepped onto the small porch and tossed the water into the front yard. What happened next shocked Alice and me. When the water hit the ground, a black cat sprang forth. It ran wildly around the house and into the pasture to the north of the house.

"Did, did, did you see that?" Alice asked in surprise.

I nodded my head. "There was no black cat lying in the grass." The yard was neatly trimmed, the grass had not yet turned green, it was still pale yellow from the winter.

"I've never in my life seen anything like that!" she said in awe.

"You've never been married to an Indian before either."

We entered the modest home. A fire crackled in the fireplace. I asked the chosen one to bless my manuscript. He agreed, revealing to me his medicine. I will not describe the process or the medicine, for it has been passed down through the ages. Its power remains with the chosen one. The next week I submitted my manuscript to the University of Nebraska Press full of confidence. It was a blessed work. It never hurts to have a little insurance.

I spend a lot of time outdoors enjoying the beauty of our little place. We have water from Lake Eufaula on three sides of our property, which adds to the beauty. Spring is beautiful here. The exploding redbuds and the crocus bring beauty to winter's dead grass. My heart dances with pleasure as I look at summer's green pasture and fall's beautiful colors. The sounds of geese flying south, both night and day. The smell of firewood on a cool, crisp evening, the smoke curling upward toward the evening sky, reminding me of how it was so many years ago when our country was young. Peace and quiet take the place of the crowded city and its traffic jams, the hustle and bustle appearing much like an anthill in perspective.

As I travel south out of the town of Eufaula, Highway 69 crosses the lake. There is water on each side of the highway. Off in the distance to the east you can see another highway bridge. This reminds me of a mini–Tampa Bay, I think of Debbie each time I leave the pretty little town. How excited she was, almost childlike, as she watched dolphins leap from the water when we crossed the long bridge that connects Tampa to Saint Petersburg.

We live a few miles south of McIntosh County, named for a distant relative. McIntosh, what a fine name. What a proud name it is in Creek history. I am so proud to have that blood flowing through my veins.

I drove to the Okmulgee Indian Baptist Church. The road to the grounds is now guarded by a locked gate. I walked past the gate toward the church grounds that held so many happy memories. Gone was the house that had stood a hundred fifty yards up the road. It had fallen down and Mother Earth had reclaimed her parcel of land. Butch and I had drunk many a Grapette beneath the shade of the porch as children. I came to the bend in the road and stopped. Grandpa's church was not there. Another little white church now stood where Grandpa's had been. It seemed smaller. The large brush arbor was gone from the south side of the church. A new one had been built on the north side but only the poles were up; the brush had yet to be gathered. I continued down the road. Only three camp houses were in use, and by the look they were not used often. The others stood rotting, including Grandma and Grandpa's house.

I came to the second bend in the road and stopped. Looking at the cemetery, I thought of my people that lay buried there. I had come to gather information, their dates of birth and death. My mind could not remember the dates, they had all died so long ago. Information gathered, I stopped and thought about each one. Remembering each of them I sighed. A hawk called from above, I looked up as he circled above me. "Rv' hv (brother)," I yelled. The hawk called again, and circled above. I smiled and waved. I looked at the campground where years ago we children ran happy and free. Now it was silent. The trees cried for a child to climb them, Mother Earth yearned for children to play in her dirt. The songbirds were silent. Who will tell the stories of the little people? Who will warn the children of the screech owl? I bade farewell to my people, we would meet again.

I stand at times in the evening looking out at the green pastures, at the cows grazing peacefully. A lone Canada goose flies by every evening honking forlornly for its lost mate. And I know how this creature feels as it lands within sight on the waters of Lake Eufaula.

I think of my friends in the Marines and wonder if they are as happy as I am at this point in their lives. It seems funny, but I miss them. I still see them.

I think about my life, and how it was so many years ago. I remember the day that Uncle Claude and Aunt Julia threw out an old Mexican woman who had come to the United States looking for work. But once there, she would not seek work and after seeing her lying around their house for months they told her to leave. I was there that day, I was twelve years old.

"I curse the Mendoza family," she yelled, pointing a finger at each of us. "You will all die horribly, this I, Hortencia, promise!" Then she turned and stormed from the porch as Uncle Claude slammed the door behind her.

Mom is a bundle of energy, and doing great. I only hope that I am in as good shape as she is when I reach her age.

Felicia and Mica visit Alice and me whenever they have a chance. Terri always runs to pah-pah when she arrives, then she runs to the swing that I made for her and hung from the big catalpa tree that stands in front of our house.

Linda and her family are doing well. Ronnie is an executive with a large company in Tulsa. Linda works at an insurance company. Diana works in sales, and Kevin is an attorney and a daddy.

Sonny and Becky have adopted a cute little boy. Robert Austin De-Graw was just a few days old when Sonny and Becky were asked if they would like to see the baby. Once again life is beautiful for them. God knows they deserve this child. I know Lance will watch over his little brother.

I miss my son. His photos adorn my house, and I think of him daily. I speak to him, because I know he is there. I remember the day, he was about four years old, when he told me that he missed me. And I, trying to comfort him, told him, "When you think of me, that means I'm thinking about you." And he felt better . . . now I feel better.

The life I shared with Debbie seems so distant, as if it never happened. I stood one evening looking at the green pastures. Suddenly I caught the fragrance of Debbie's perfume. It was strong. I knew she was with me. I thanked her for bringing Alice to me. I told her that this was the happiest time of my life. I speak to the invisible world because I know that it exists. That is the difference between the Indian and the white man. The white man prays to an unseen God. We pray also, but we also ask the spirits to guide us. We use medicine for assistance, and we are one with the spirit world.

It's strange that everything I ever wanted has come to be. A true love. My children and grandchildren doing well. A farm, which Debbie and I had always wanted, is now my home. I wanted to retire early so that I might write stories for and about my people, and that has come to be. My guardian spirit has blessed me. I do not have riches in the form of shiny new cars, or a million-dollar home. My riches are about me. My wife, my children and grandchildren. The land that lives beneath our feet, that sustains us while we live and holds us when we die. These are my riches. What more does a man need?

When I make the drive to Tulsa I visit Debbie, Lance, and Wayne at the cemetery. I know it is only their bodies that are there, their spirits have gone on, yet a part of me says go to where they lie, and I go. I will never forget them.

This place where I live has brought me closer to my Indian heritage. I travel the land of Alexander Posey, the famed Creek author and poet. I have visited Bald Hill where he lived. To my surprise I found that he knew my great-grandfather, Temiye Kernels. Temiye also knew Chitto Harjo, better known as Crazy Snake.

Last year Alice made Terri an Indian dress. Alice, Mom, Terri, and I attended the powwow held in Eufaula in September. I watched proudly as my two-year-old granddaughter danced to the beat of the singing and the drums. She was shy at first, but the desire to dance won out. I thought of Little Grandma and I smiled at my little bundle of energy as she stomped the ground with her little moccasins.

On 4 March 1995 Bryson Taylor Ball entered the world. Micaela had given birth to my grandson. I stood next to my son-in-law, Preston. We stared at the dark-skinned baby with the full head of black hair. Preston was white-skinned, he has Cherokee and Blackfoot blood but doesn't know the exact degree. We were surprised that the baby boy looked so Indian. As I watched Mica hold her son with love, I suddenly realized what Oscar had felt at the birth of Felicia. My eyes watered also. I had lived the past, now as I looked at mother and child I saw the future. I wished Dad was there, and my Waleeta, Little Grandma, everyone that I had loved and lost. Then I realized that they *were* there, I could feel them all about me and happiness filled my heart.

The hawk calls to me, and I to him. He visits me daily, this little sparrow hawk. At times he sits within reach, turning his head this way and that as I speak to him. Other times he sits perched on a limb, not a dozen paces from me. When he departs he always soars high above me on the four winds, as if wanting me to follow. Deep in my heart I know that someday, when I lie down for the last time, I shall rise to him, and together we will soar on the four winds over the mountain to the invisible world that awaits.

I am not torn between God and the Great Spirit, for they are both my fathers, as they have always been, even before I was aware of them. Had I not seen Joseph Smoke I might not have readily accepted the beliefs of my people. The stories of transformation from man to wild beast are no more absurd than Jonah and the whale. The beliefs of my people are founded in the openness to accept the spirit world. The earth, our mother; the sky, our father. How beautiful a concept, how pure. Religion . . . there is no right or wrong. Whether it be God Almighty or Allah, it is paramount to accept the fact that we are not alone on this earth.

The spirit that has watched over me all my life has blessed me. The good times and the sad touch everyone. It is life. Endure, then weep, endure, and be rewarded, endure and rejoice, endure and learn, coming full circle . . . eternal.

They call to me, my two fathers. For they know they are within my soul. I . . . Son of Two Bloods.

Winners of the North American Indian Prose Award

Claiming Breath
Diane Glancy

They Called It Prairie Light:
The Story of Chilocco Indian School
K. Tsianina Lomawaima

Son of Two Bloods
Vincent L. Mendoza

All My Sins Are Relatives
William S. Penn

Completing the Circle
Virginia Driving Hawk Sneve